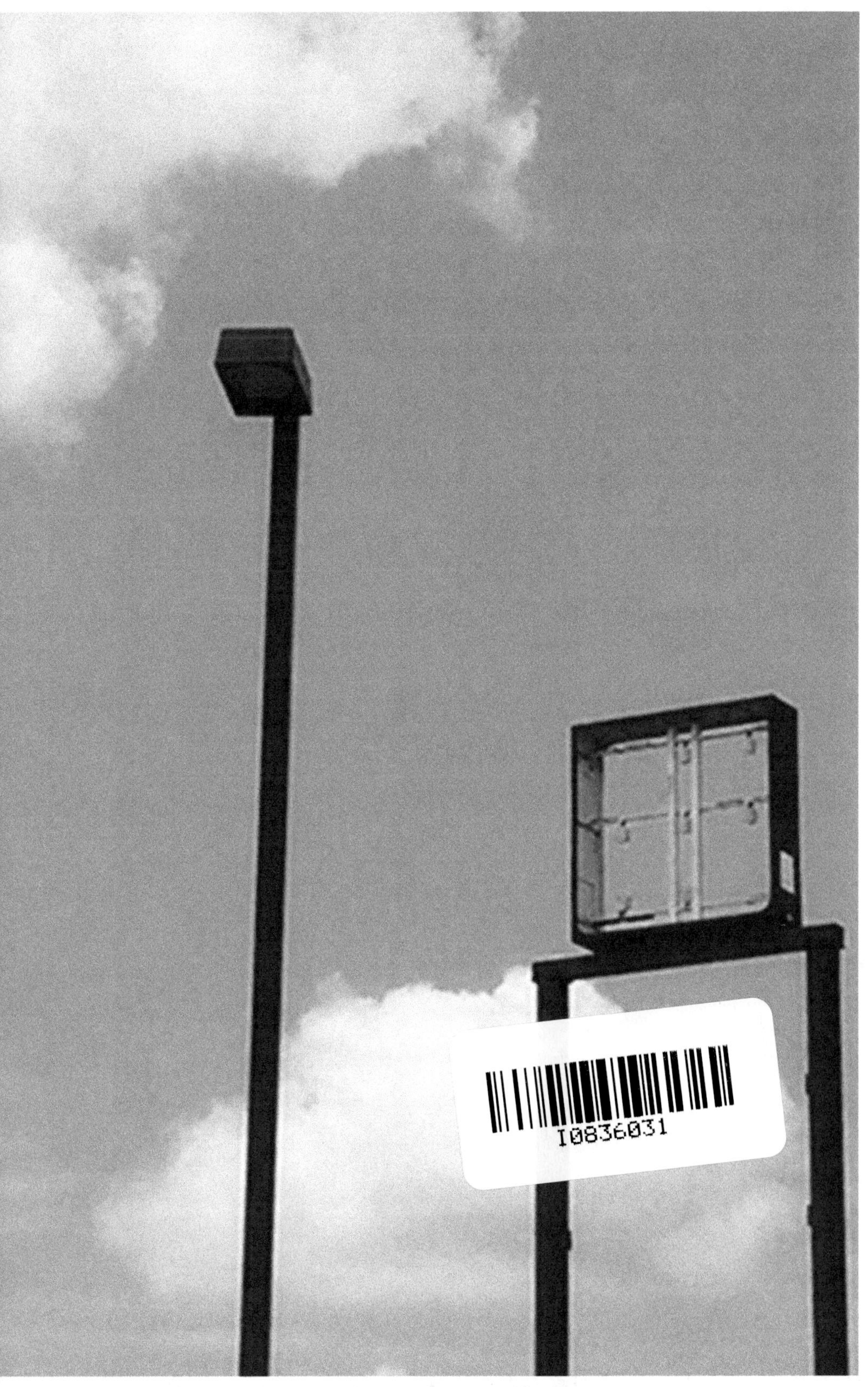
I0836031

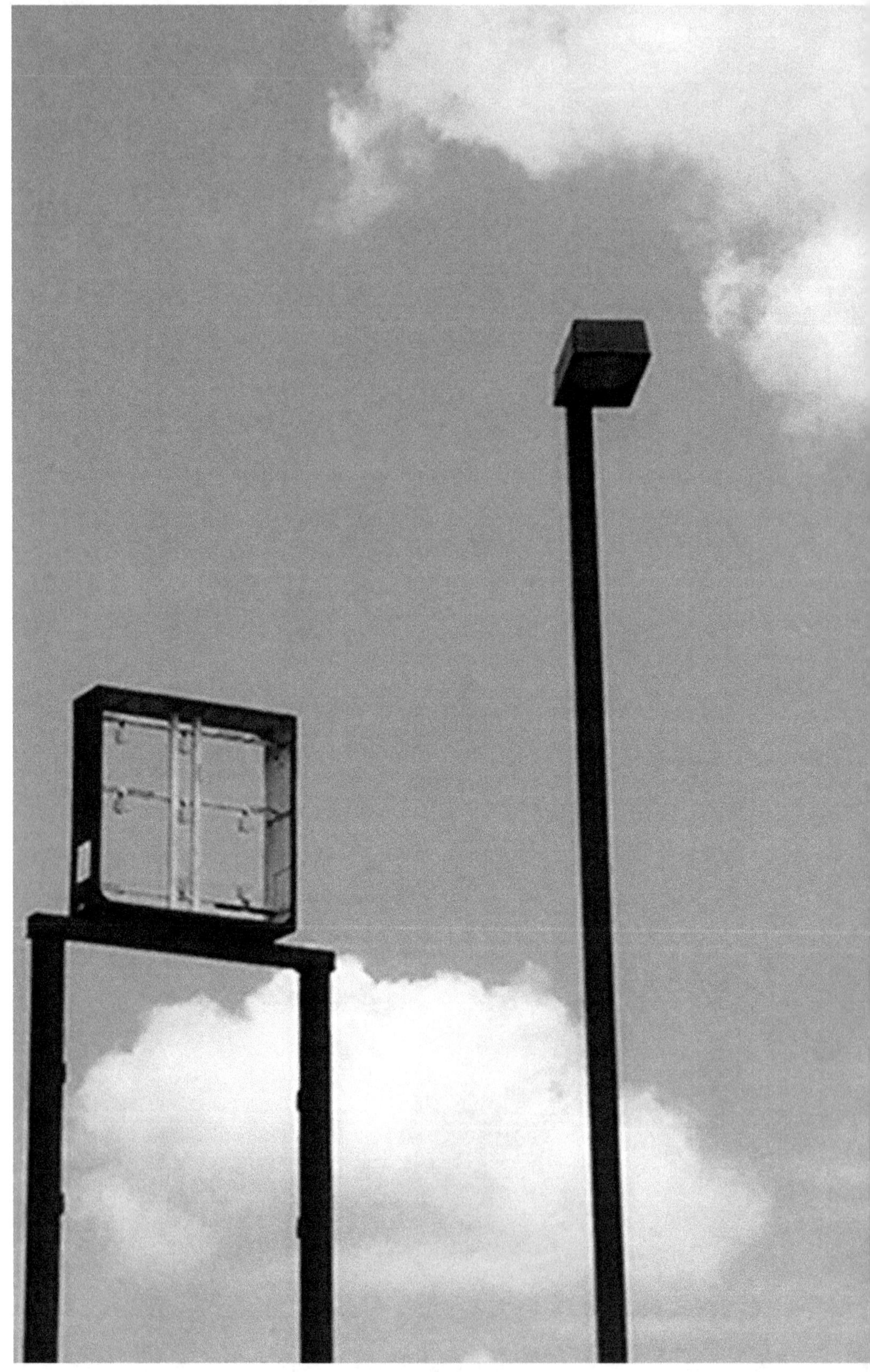

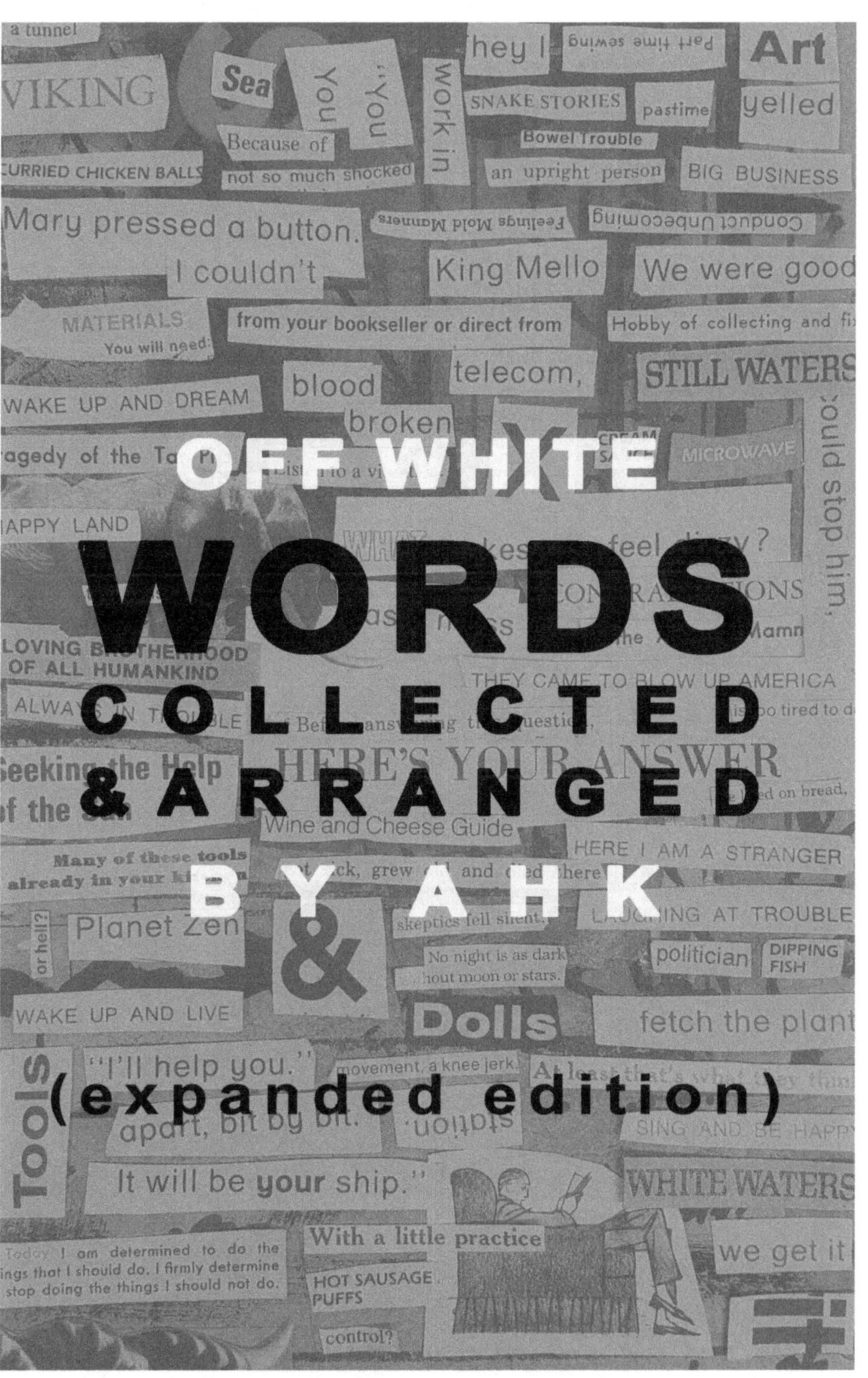
OFF WHITE
WORDS
COLLECTED
& ARRANGED
BY AHK
(expanded edition)

we are proud of this book and we think it is perfect for everyone.

PUBLISHED BY
TRIANGLE NONPROFIT PUBLISHING

Find out how you can get involved at TRIANGLE-NONPROFIT-PUBLISHING.ORG

ISBN 9781737475507

ABOUT THIS BOOK

THE WORLD WE LIVE IN GOES UP AND DOWN

while THE SIMPLEST solutions

grow like trees from the ground

There you have it.

NO FURTHER READING

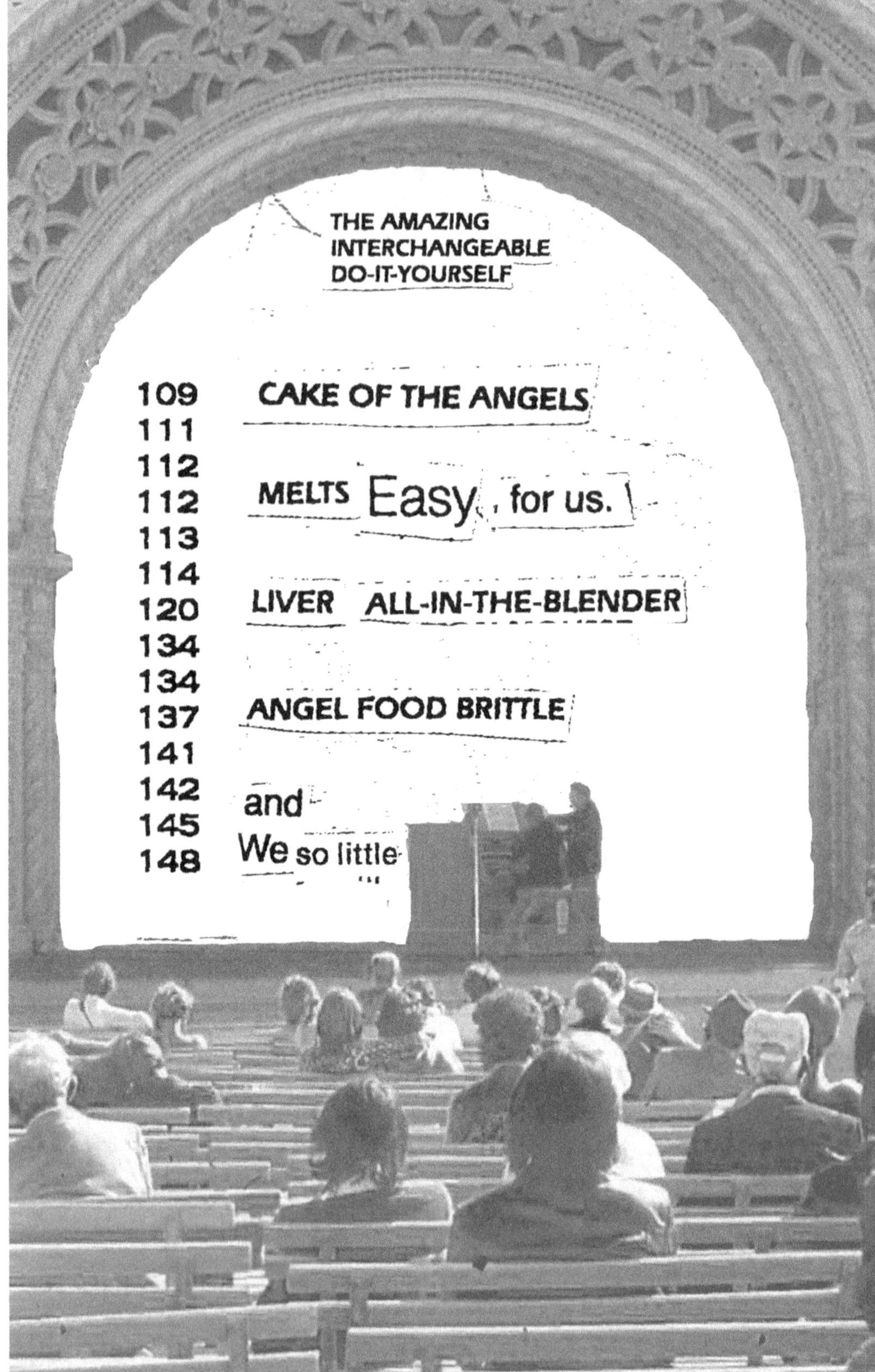
THE AMAZING
INTERCHANGEABLE
DO-IT-YOURSELF
109 CAKE OF THE ANGELS
111
112
112 MELTS Easy , for us.
113
114
120 LIVER ALL-IN-THE-BLENDER
134
134
137 ANGEL FOOD BRITTLE
141
142 and
145
148 We so little

The Art of Floating through.

Plexiglas Beverages

Halcyon pages.

Butterfly' PUFFS

Invisible freedom

and other colors

and Sauces

worn by

dolls and puppets

impromptu Condiments

SHRIMP AND DIP

mud-covered blob.

Painting stripes on cars.

This is really an art.

the mess they make,

in the forebrain, midbrain and the Window Pane

gaze into it, call out its name,

War-Between-the-States

time to paint.

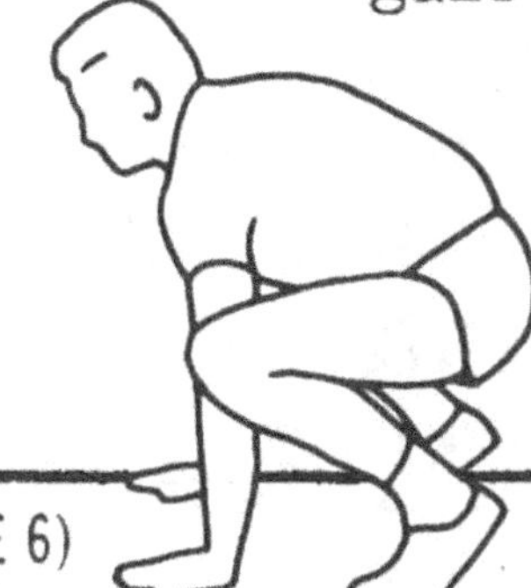

(FIGURE 6)

the reason for its being.

more
-CHEESE

EASY CHEESE

BAKED ORANGE
SWEET HOT
White Faith SEEDS
CHEESE-STUFFED CHEESE
AND CHEESE
on everything

You will find
WILD AND LONG
satisfaction
CON QUESO.

They wore
WILD PONIES
for a normal sexual relationship.

UNBELIEVABLE PIE
Several dozen
poodle owners swear by

a little different
and always happy to give
for a little while

I think I may say that
cake
has become a way of life.

Art of The
Boat Farm
Goes to College

ADULT EDUCATION
Time-Saving Recipes
Auto Raising
Reweavingings
children never seem to get enough
SHOESTRINGS of the colors they see,
Freezing

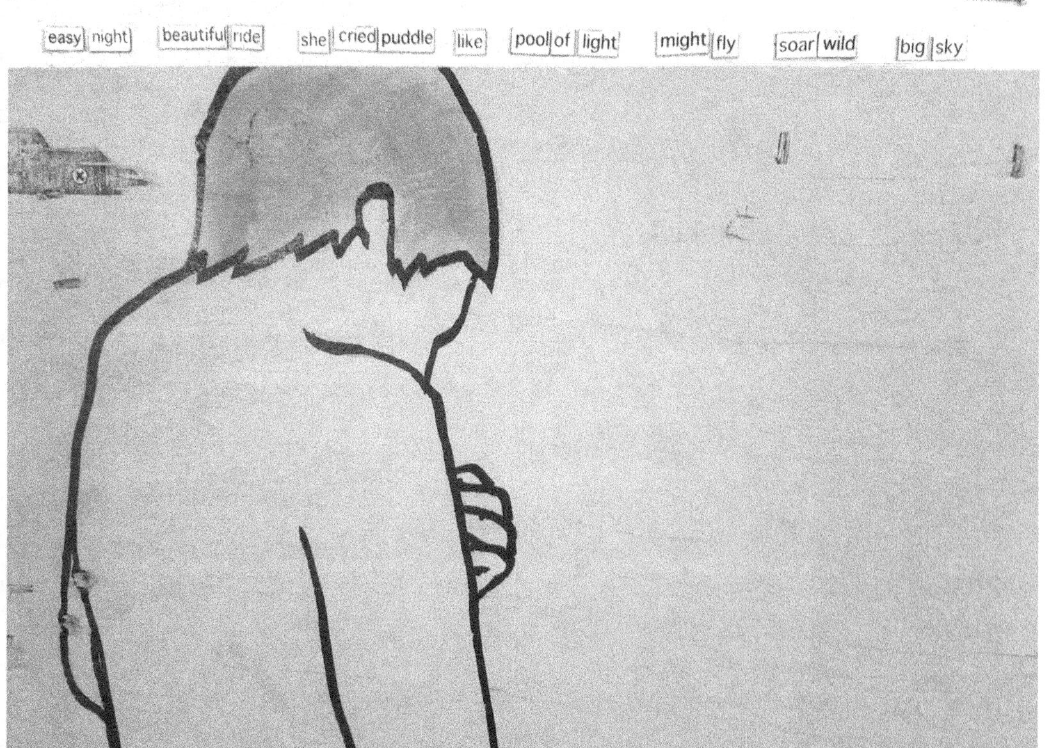

at

Work

for all mankind.

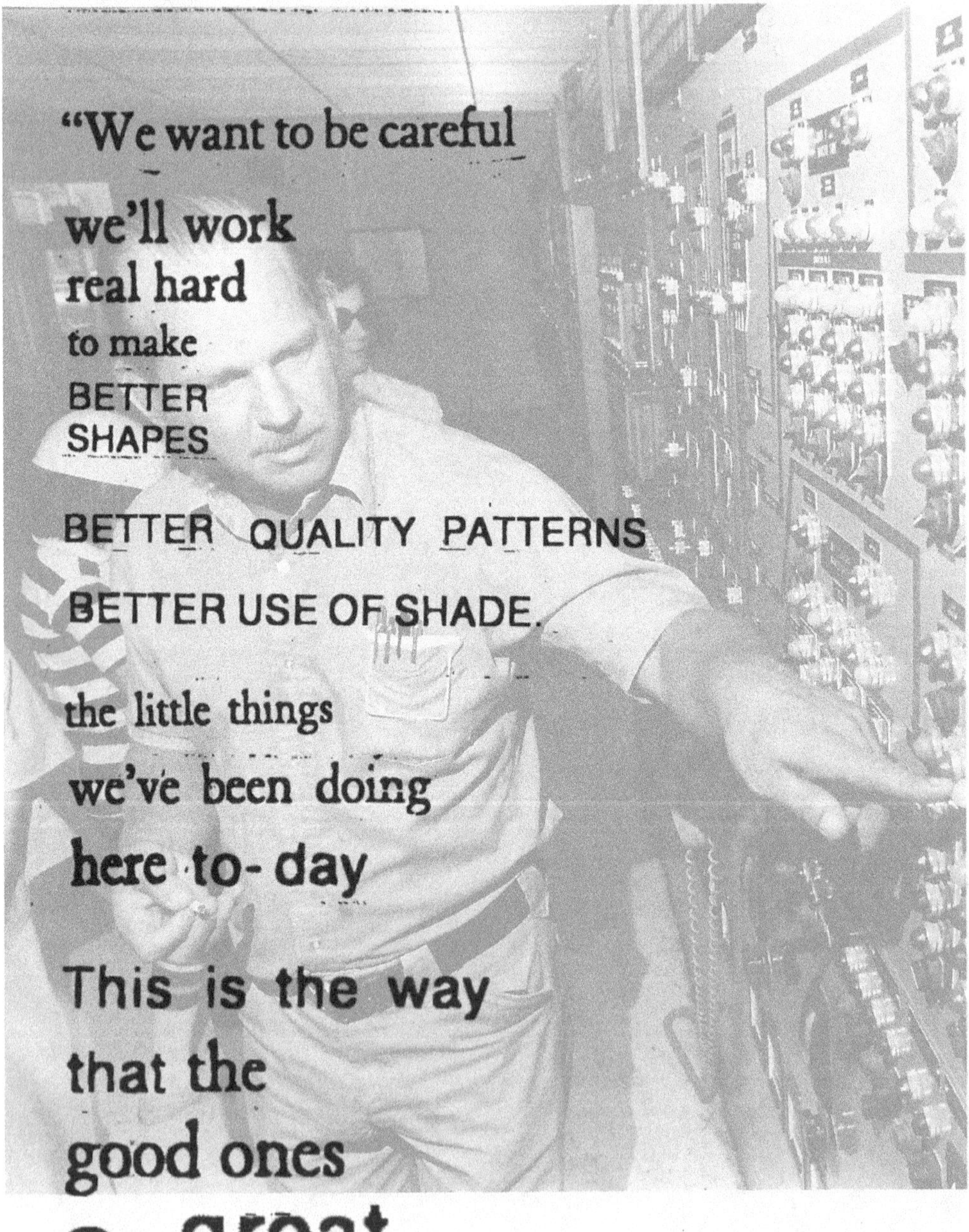

"We want to be careful

we'll work
real hard
to make
BETTER
SHAPES

BETTER QUALITY PATTERNS

BETTER USE OF SHADE.

the little things
we've been doing
here to-day

This is the way
that the
good ones
Go great

Look,

Love and War go hand in hand.

he believed,

Each person has dreams,

and fat on their backs.

dying slowly, fast.

Every small child is

blinded by the smog,

it has invaded our

golden days

Current Happenings

All around us

there's nothing

we can see

Look!

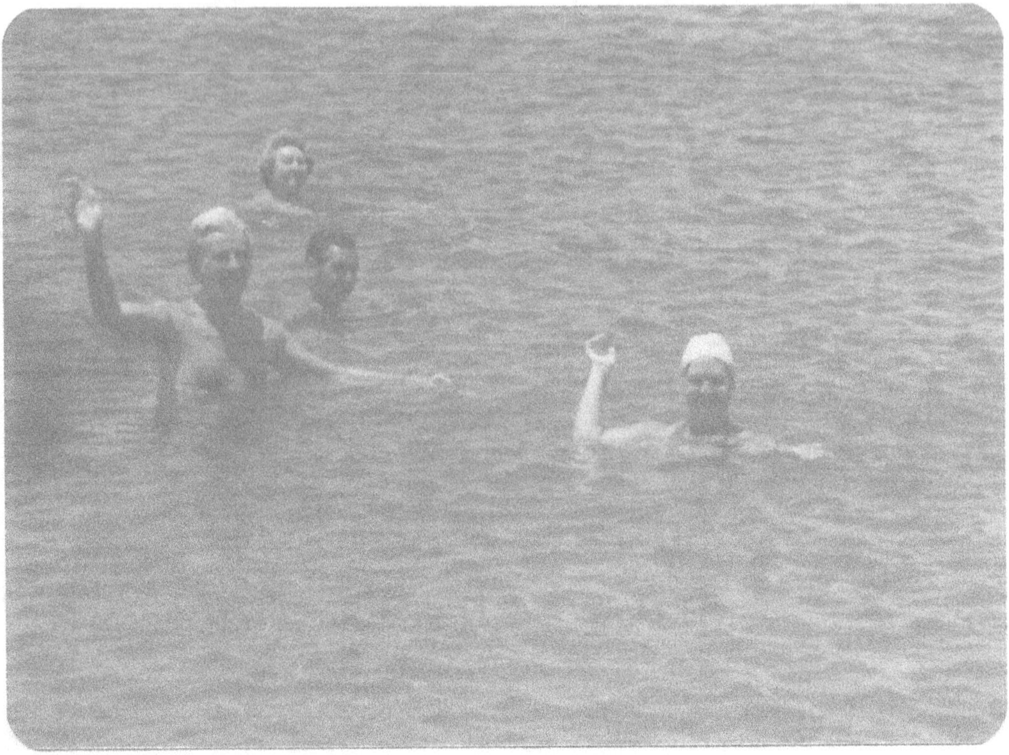

Some butchers will donate animal hearts to A LOST ART.

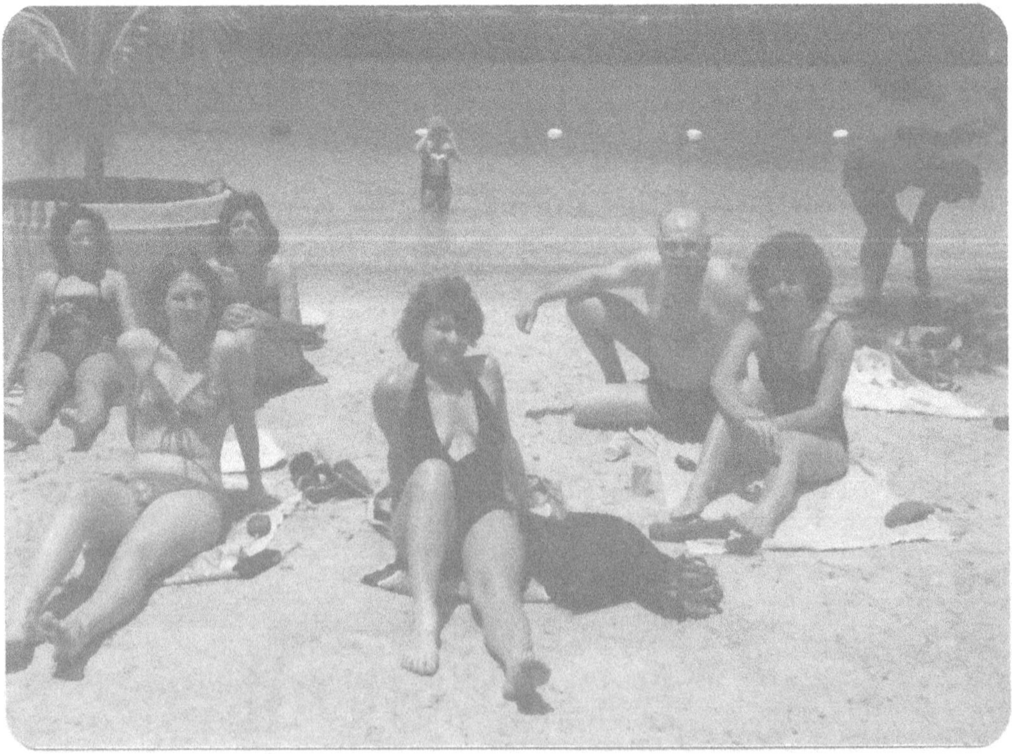

because each other.

When magic works, as it sometimes does,

There is music in the world

and the Future is young and deeply in love

It is easy to see that

THE FRUIT of the tree

was once the heat of the sun.

Everything that has
happened has happened to the two of us,

and that is why it matters.

Many robots,
Honor and Obey
give birth to their young
TO GET THE SAME

lucky Whites,
Born right,
wonder drugs
heart-shaped
Christ-

There was no danger
in their sky,

Freedom
too
Must Surely Die.

99.9999 percent are Gods Looking for the Kind of Help You Can Give Them

HUMAN RELATIONSHIPS

mind The moon

N IN SOCIETY

work on growth

play in The wave

Alter All you want to

you know you want to

All YOU

Super

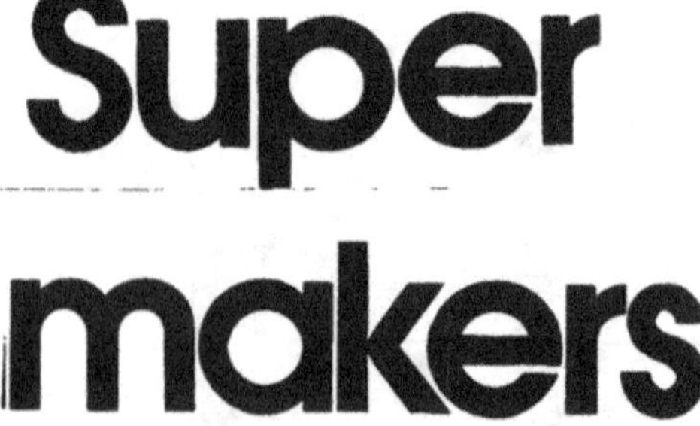

makers

Lifting depression

Do No Miracles
Fear Freedom
Con the Community

LIVING WITH OTHERS

Decay the spirit
you Strange
Men of rank with
Malignant brains
Mapping the End

Could you be a

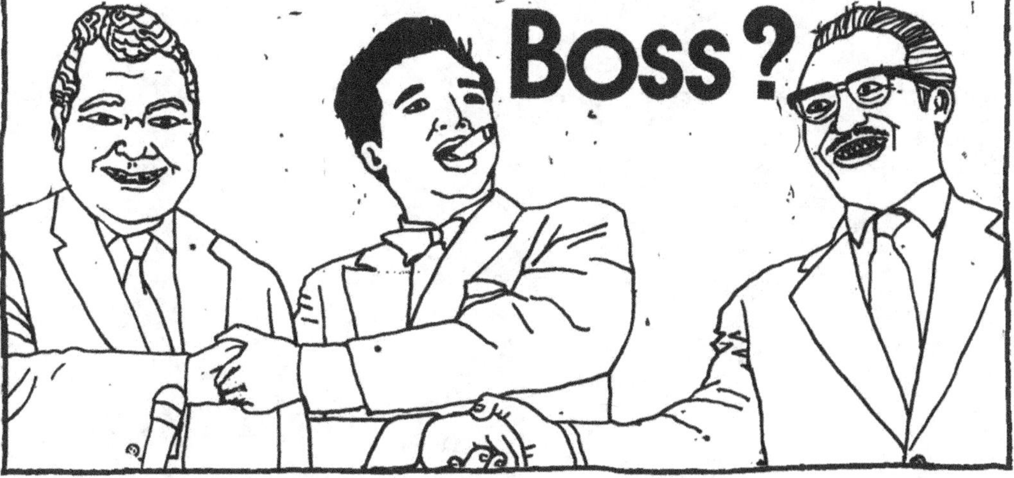

where the weather is made.

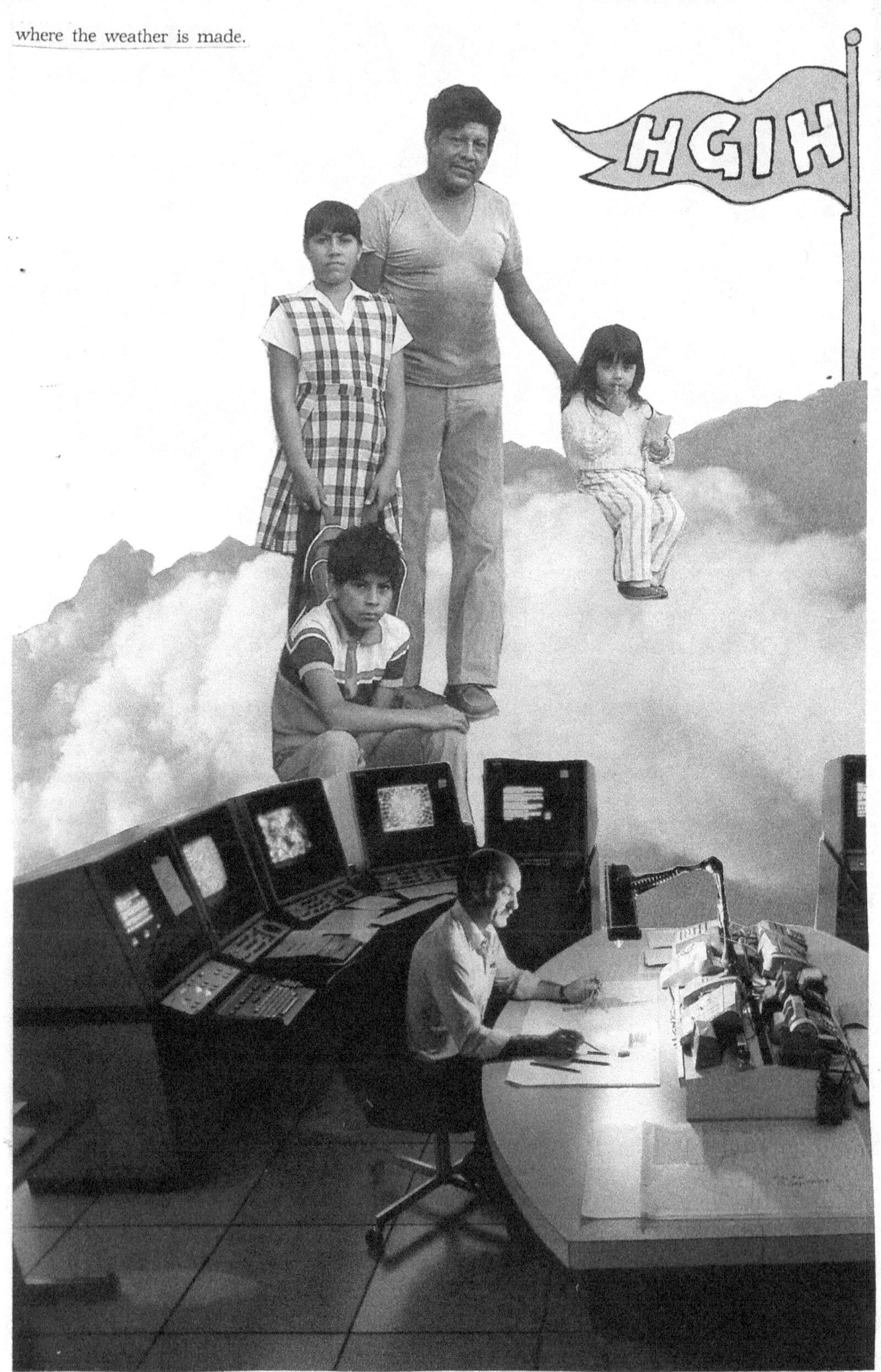

In our world of air and skies
in this constant parade of dark and light,
with stars on all sides ,
you get new eyes and time to die.
There is nowhere to hide.
and the moon swings through,
and the sun swings through,
and the Earth swings through too,
almost at the same time –
and all is clear
and all is true
in the eternal moment
In the middle of the night

I hope this book will help you see,
the great beauty, the unfathomable mystery
and recognize you're in deep
we are all a great part
of The same tiny thing
in exactly this same place
stretching
through
eternity.

skeletons are never together.

their fuel tanks might explode.

Whether the appeal of

Civil War

SMÖRGÅSBORD

or a good deal more,

The fire spread

IN COUNTLESS HOMES

GHOST TOWNS

TRAVELING AROUND

They **will** remain so

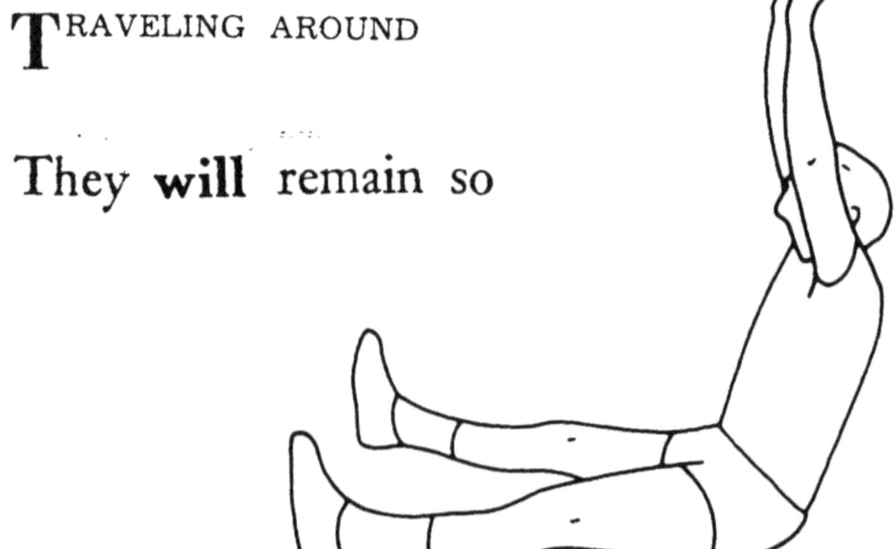

FOR ever

Stuffed Animal

Walking Circus

Dog Doll

Ship Shop

Print Plant

Miniature Giver

Sign Farmer

Private Poodle

Party Restorer

Carving Letters

Into Icons

Model Metal

in Repairs

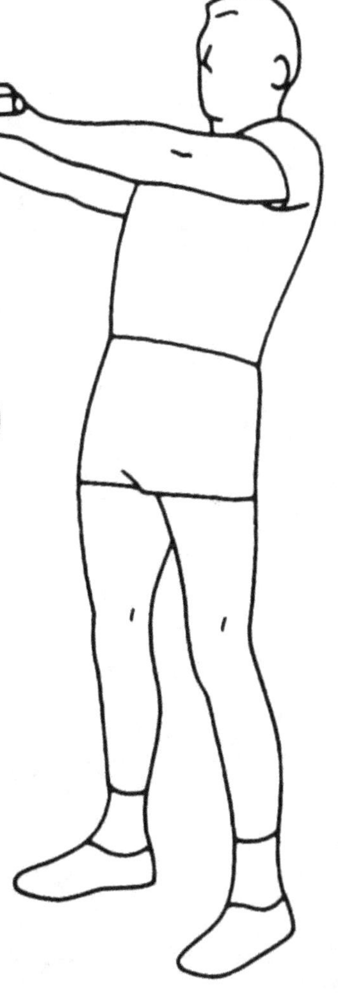

Little talent is required for this

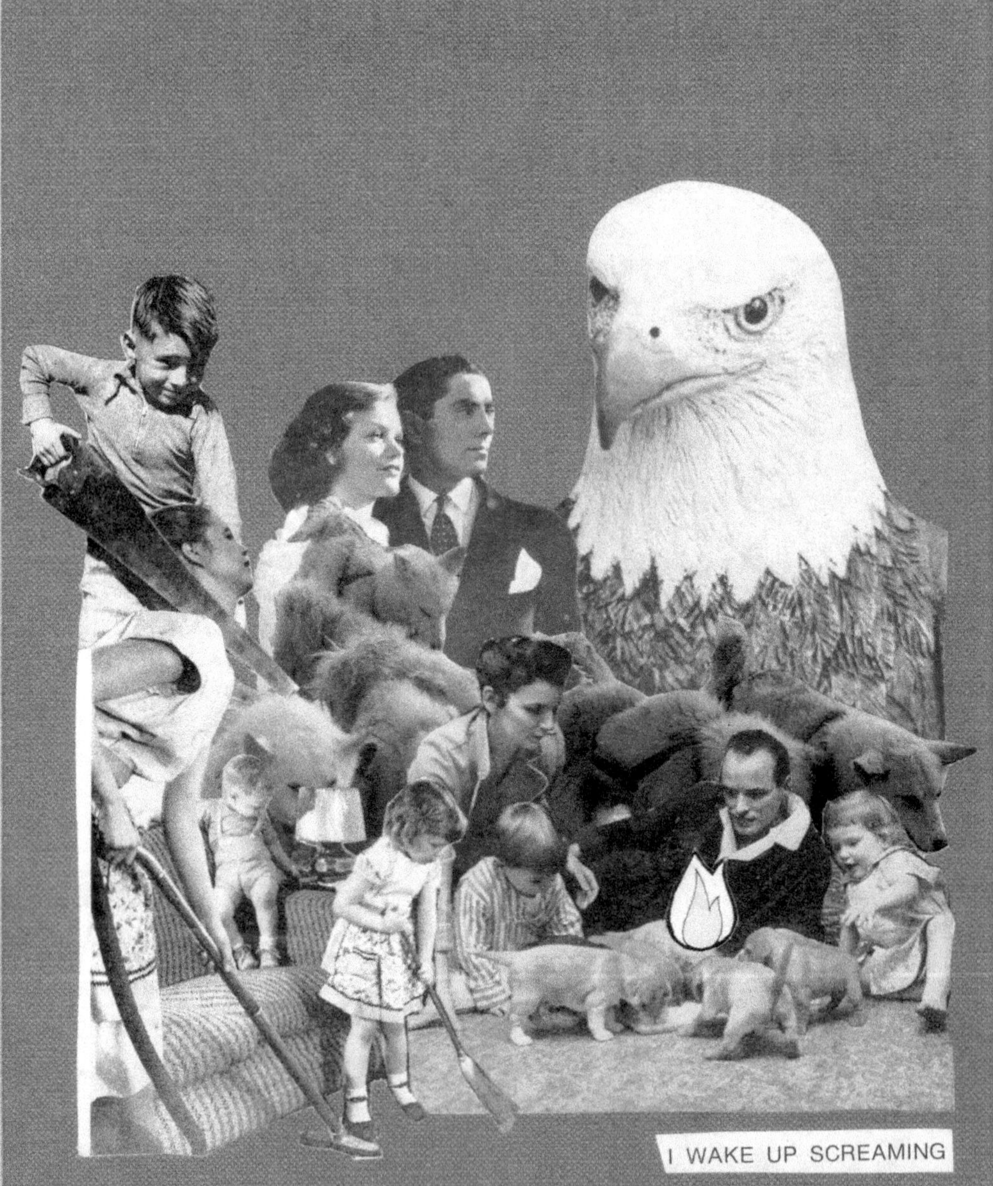
I WAKE UP SCREAMING

What I Know About The PROPHECY OF THE

PRETTY GIRLS AND PRETTY HORSES

got away Into The Sunset,

From that day to this,

• Nerves and Telephone Wires ....

'INTO THE SUNSET'-

AND THE horses rode away

INTO THE SUNSET ....

RIVER ON THE RIVER

SEVEN TALL TEXANS.

Inside and Outside of Me..

HORSE upon his horse Riding INTO THE SUNSET

Maybe there was a red balloon

IN A LONELY TOMB.

Maybe you have even dug for it, or wanted to,

for its pretty girls and pretty horses

"Soapsuds" – into the Sunset!

STARS FELL ON

THE COWBOY CASTLE

The parakeets and parrots flew over

the VALLEY OF TEARS in swarms.

they began eating on the colonists.

which all said they never wanted to leave again.

LIKE ANGELS OF MERCY

NEITHER BLOODY NOR DIRTY

POST TOASTIES AND CONDENSED MILK

SOURDOUGH BISCUITS IN THE PAN-

ROPE IN THE SKY

It was the way of human life

and everything looked pretty good for awhile.

IN TEXAS

The day your life became a dream...

The dogs ate **hot dogs,**

the food of the future human race

Awkward Silences ate the men and women.

life-long affection

A COWBOY'S RELIGION

Illusion is Delusion

home becomes a prison

wedding rings **a** circle to contain the soul

to wash the baby or to drown him,

We sometimes mix this up

monkeys (above)

suffering from

a part of human life

that

happens

To most of us,

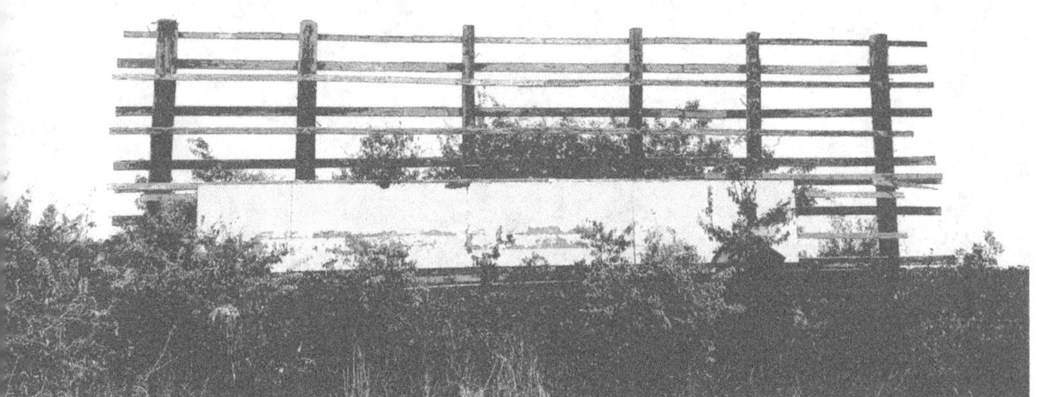

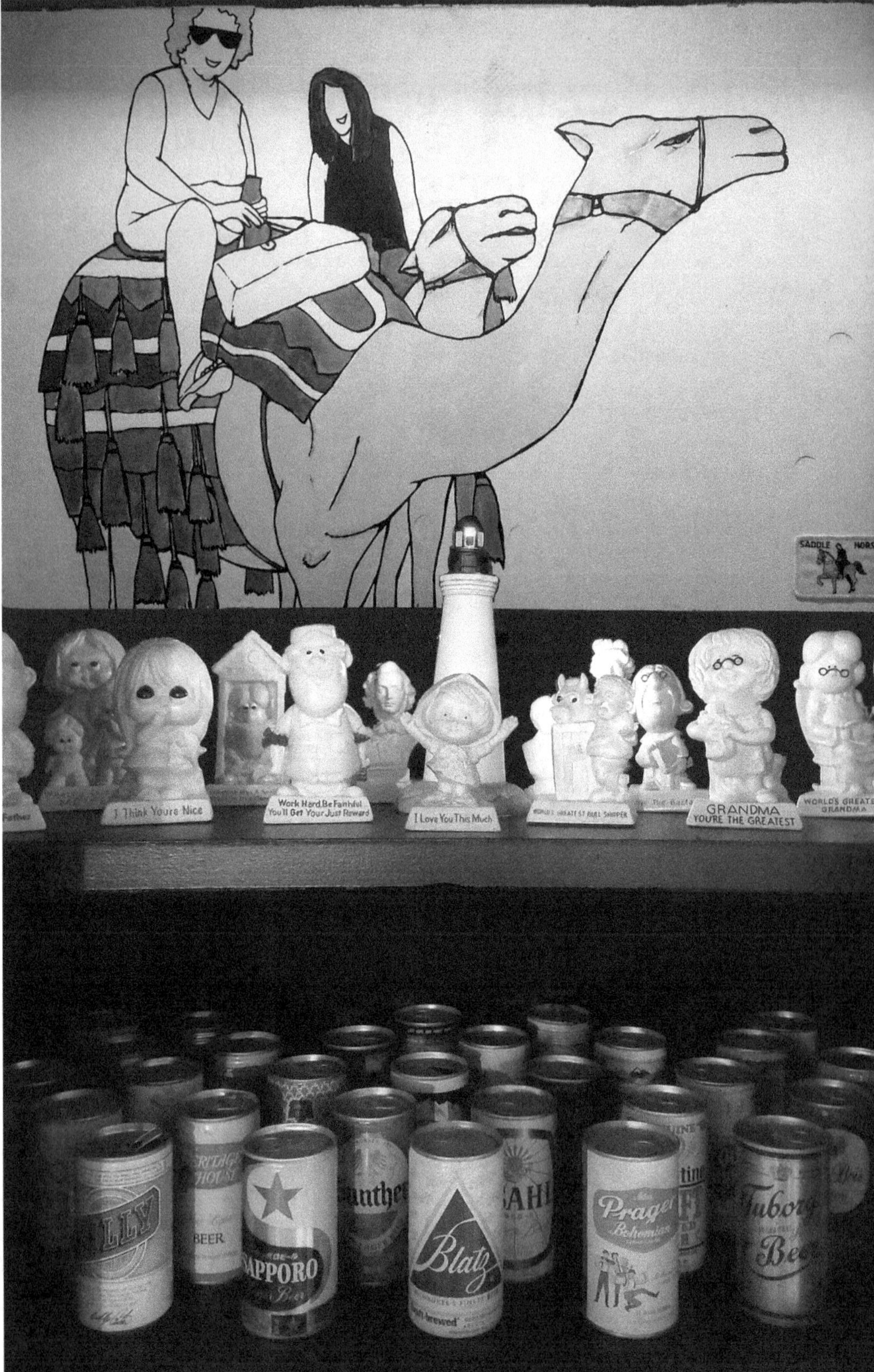
I Think Youre Nice
Work Hard Be Faithful
You'll Get Your Just Reward
I Love You This Much
GRANDMA
YOU'RE THE GREATEST
SAPPORO
Blatz
Prager
Bohemian
BEER

"What's it for?" he wanted to know.

they wouldn't want if they knew

it is made on the machine loom.

found in tombs and messed up.

from other lands, from other days.

When we look at the sad-walls and ceilings;

We would rock with laughter if we caught sight
of a reason for being.

I make my living

This may seem like a ridiculously obvious idea today,

but

MOST OF THE MANY WONDERS OF LIFE ON EARTH

are made by

A HAND

Miles Down

BENEATH

the Sea

THE CATCHER IN THE DEEP

captured undersea

In the early TIME

by **THE AUTHORS** and the Editors of LIFE,

Seeking The sky for which she was designed.

She is usually bewildered by the hearts of men

The **Men** with **DESIGNS**

and A PILE OF PLANS

SEARCHING FOR new **Dooms**

Converting time
into problems
BY PUSH BUTTON

coffin INCORPORATED.
NEW YORK

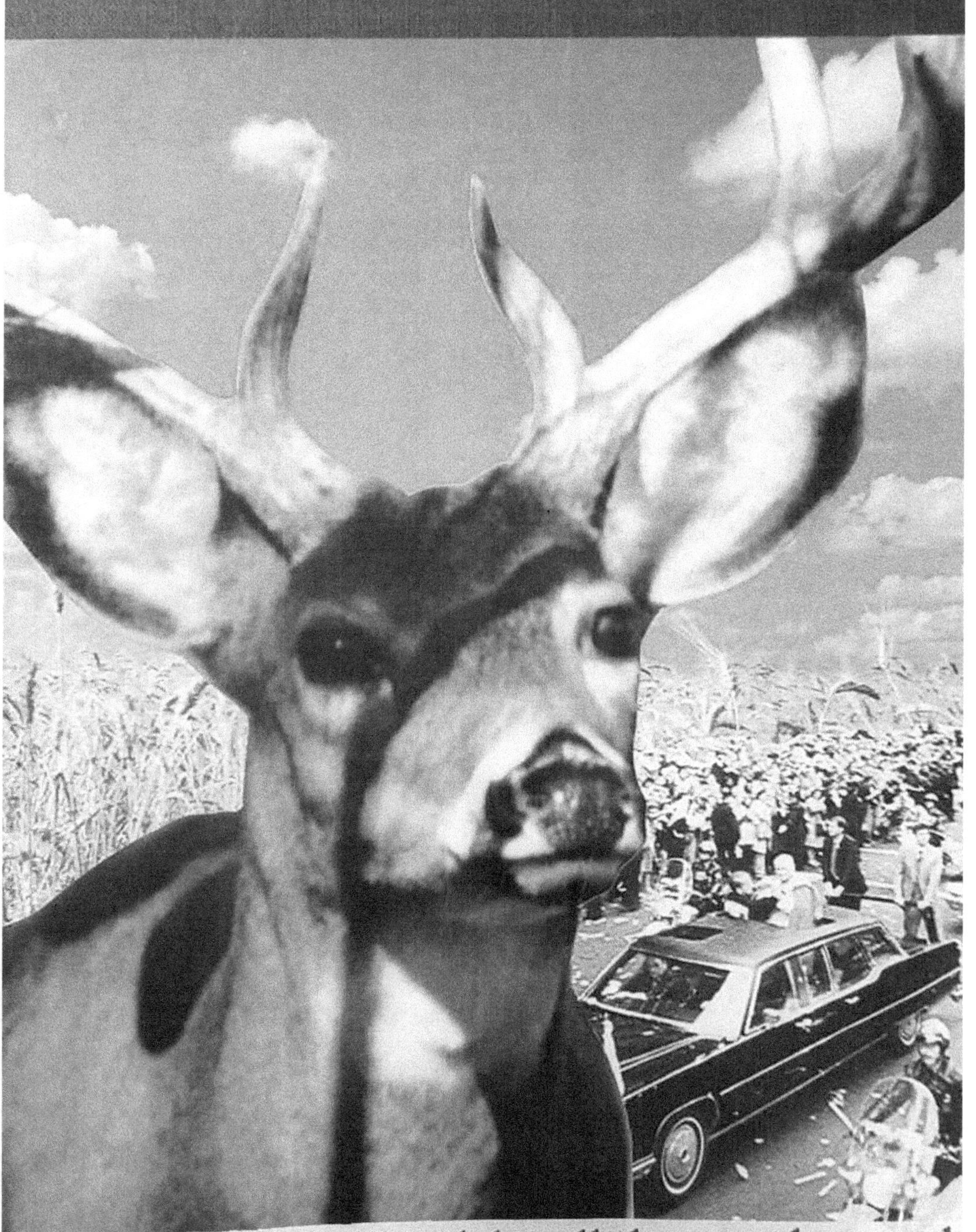
Surrounded from birth by all the wonders and

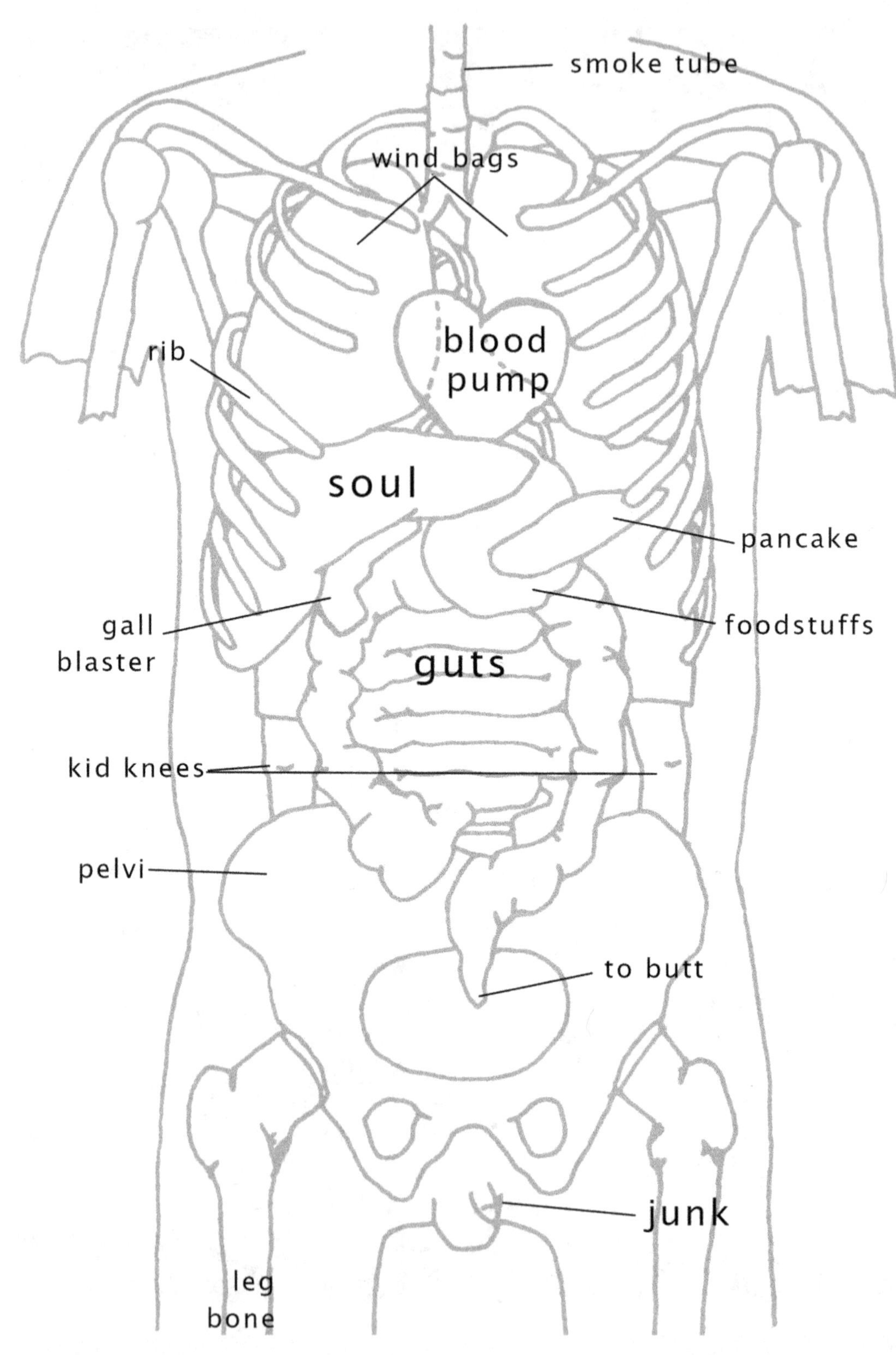
smoke tube
wind bags
blood
pump
rib
soul
pancake
foodstuffs
gall
blaster
guts
kid knees
pelvi
to butt
junk
leg
bone

–What I Know About My Heart.

It Is a Pump.

My Heart Is a Pump

no matter how **strong** the feeling of good will toward men springs from inside

• My Heart is a muscle that pumps blood around and around

It travels through tunnels inside the body

so I can wave hello to you.

• Can You Do That? ....

-I Learned Something New About My Heart.

Can You Do That?

"Look out!" and wonder.
The night sky is a sight of beauty
We know it is true because
it seems to be

"Be a guest at your own party"

If you let go of the string,

We can see

we should make up

the universe

as we breathe.

Now we begin to understand

that he is in a trance.

I followed him.

and when I did

I realized that I myself had been

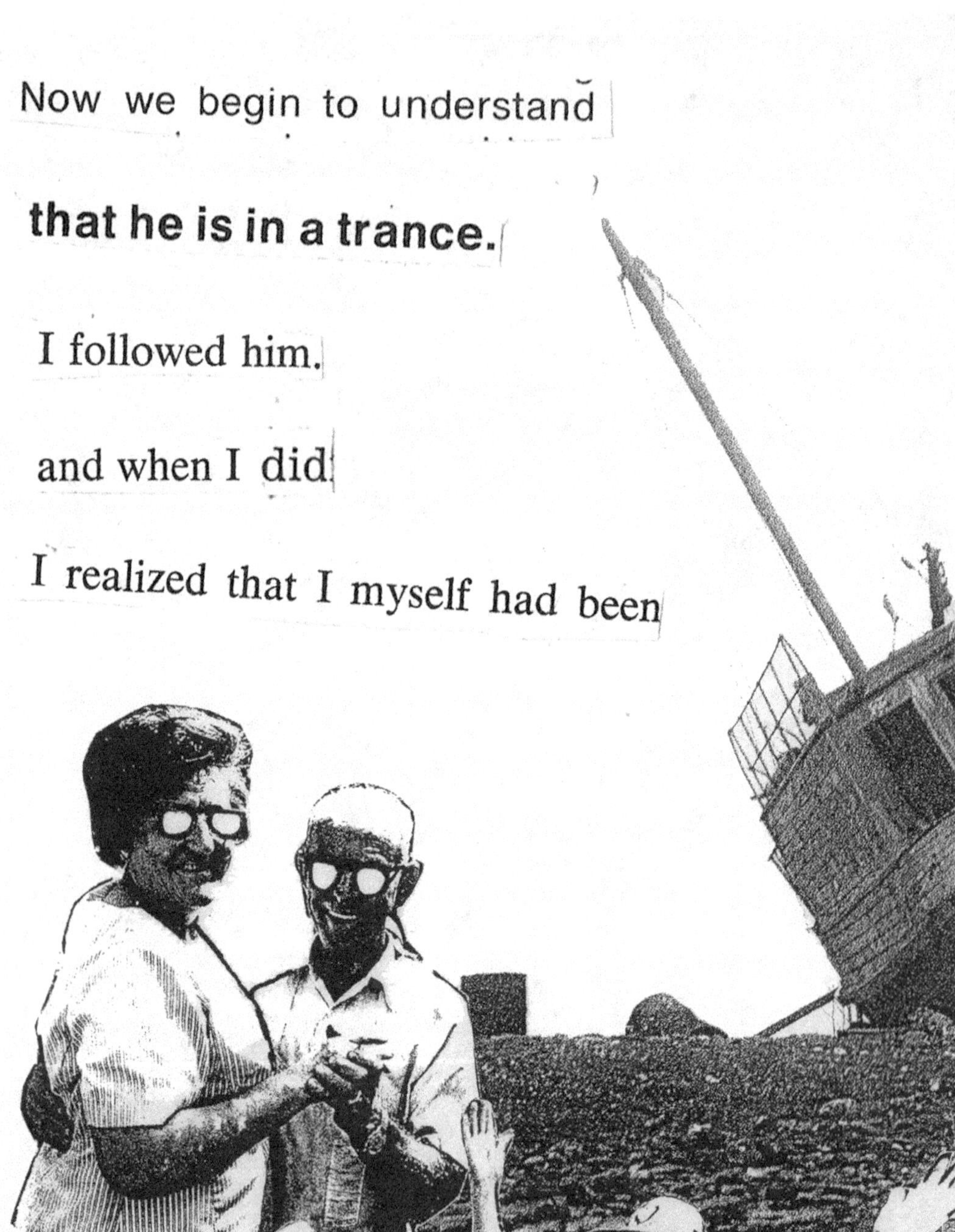

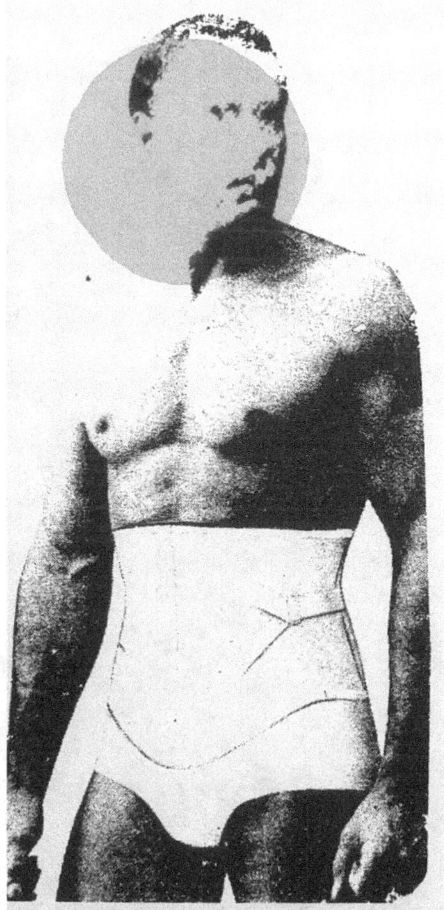

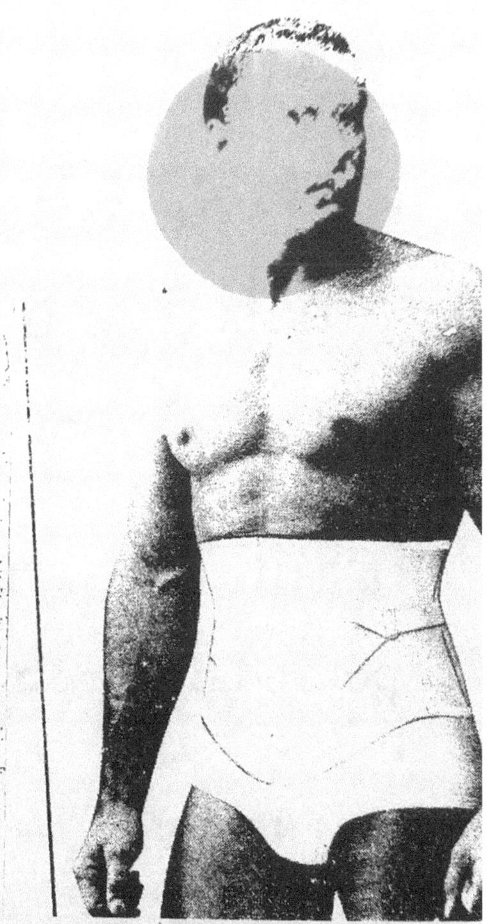

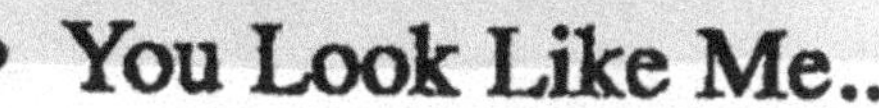

Look in a mirror.

Can you tell me what you see?

You Look Like Me

My body is like your body

We have the same number of eyes."

• Cut them Out.......................

.... Send a Message •

there was a big bang

FOUNTAIN OF LIFE

created and destroyed

at the edge of a swift stream

It ran to extremes,

poured down on all living things

WELLSPRINGS OF **Water Mains**

Mighty floodwaters
flowing inexorably

Waterways of industry

tumbling turbulently toward the sea,

Rivers of **Brain Waves**
slowed to a drip.
leak through the cracks
into large rooms and passageways.
and in so many
different places
Everywhere on this
FLOATING Maze
the water descends.

Babies Feel
the Influence

it cuts gorges

to wash away
their sins;

points of view.

birthday
Blues

BRIGHT
ORANGE
Soups
moved

DARK BLUE
hearts
moved too.

The story you
have just read is true.

we know it.

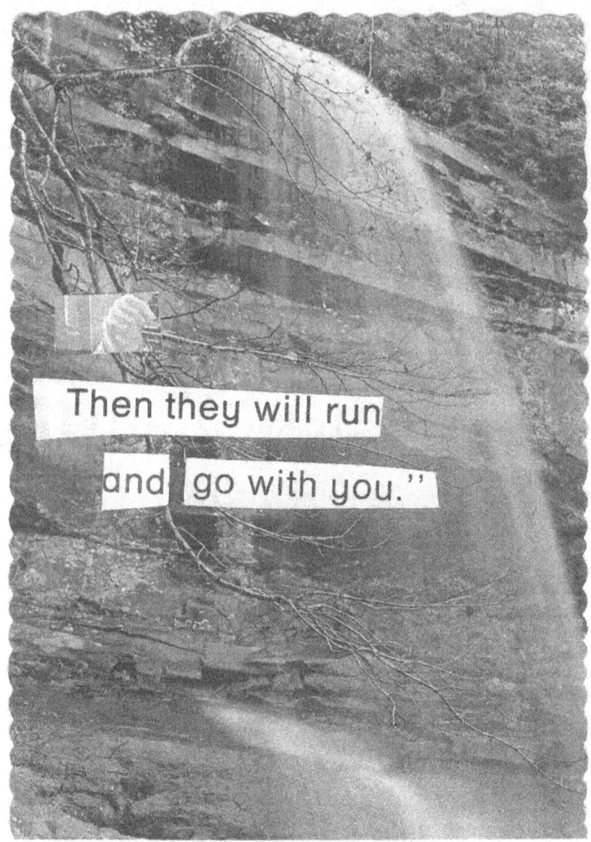

Rainbow Falls - Great Smoky Mountains National Park photo John Earl

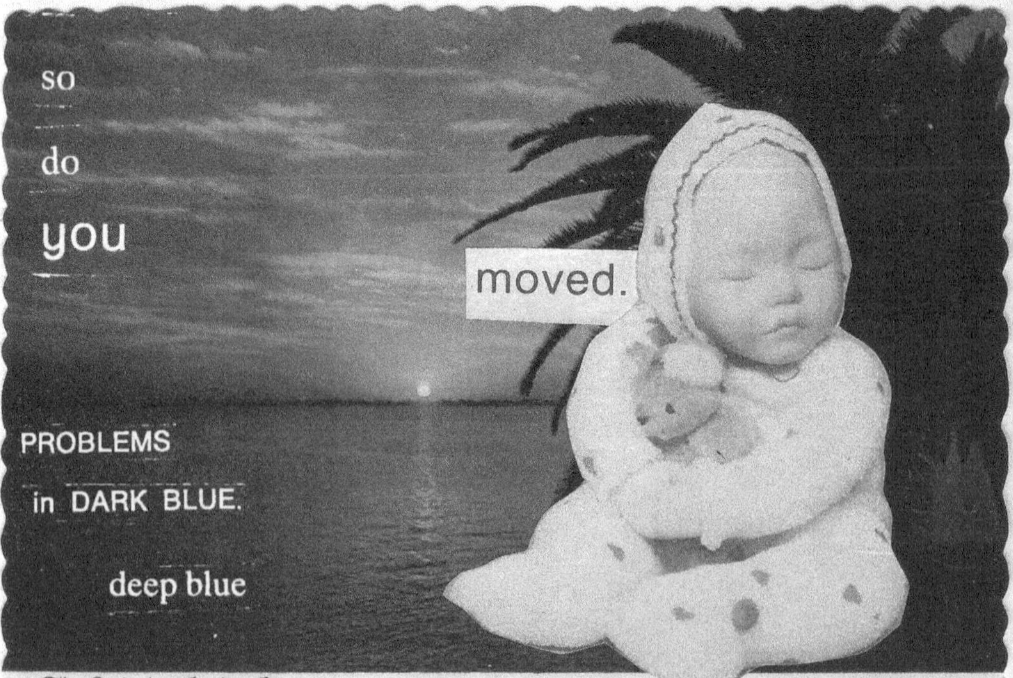

so
do
you
moved.

PROBLEMS
in DARK BLUE.
deep blue

The End of a Perfect Day Photo by H. Hannau

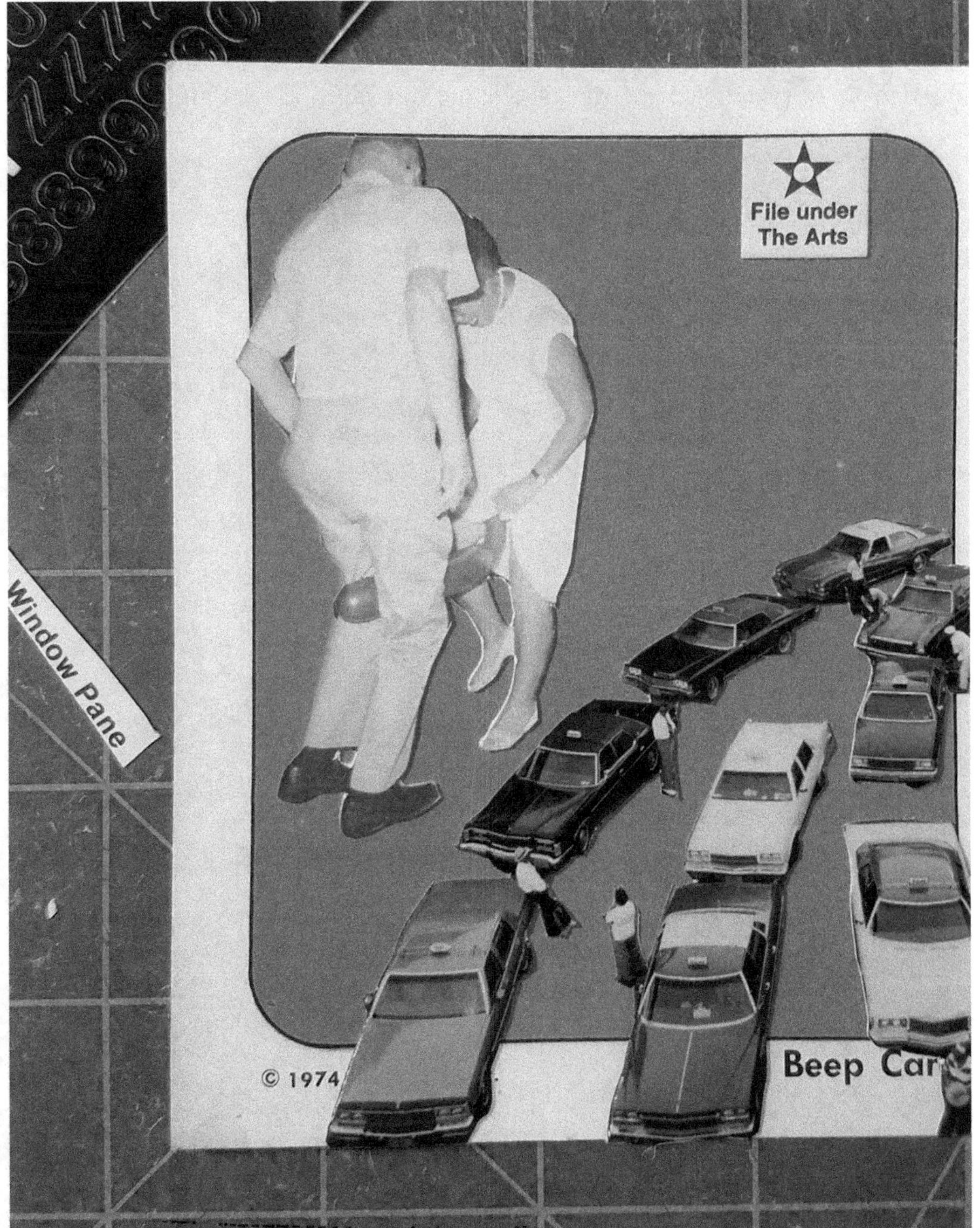

How to Play Beep Beep

MATERIALS You will need: a rectangle ring, consciousness of the Sticky Street a large piece of the surface of the earth, a piece of drawing paper, a black crayon, food pieces from different kinds of houses, future happiness, an orange crayon and *It Takes a Lot of People*, wives and children, Filmstrip, rhythm instruments, scissors paste, red fire engines, Beep Beep Cards, animal hearts **& HOT TUBS**

crumble between your fingers. the mysterious and the unfathomable.

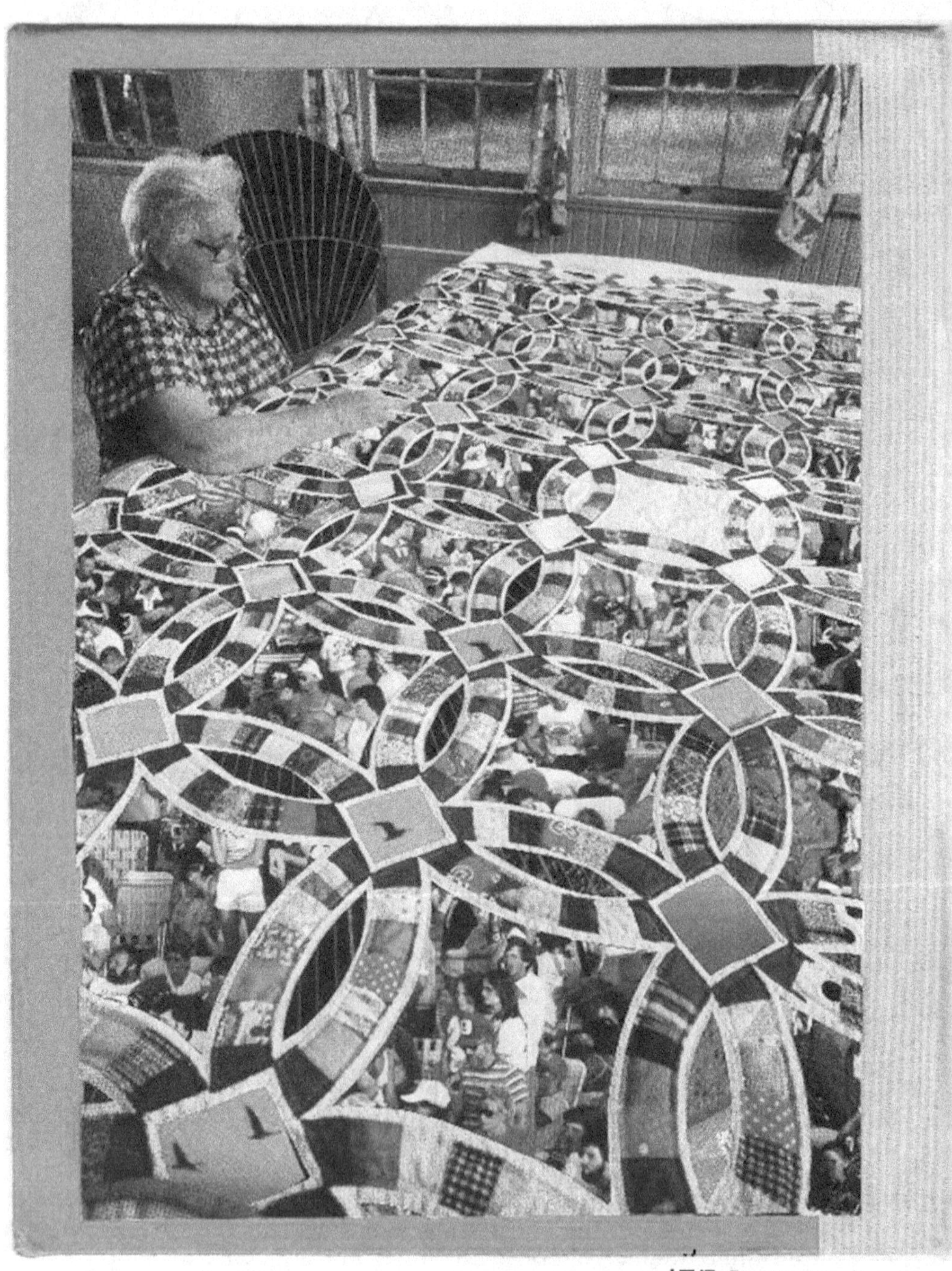

Bake a big batch at the void

maybe you're a Boss yourself!

become addicted to the
magical principle of
Making money
for money.
selling Everything
All the time.

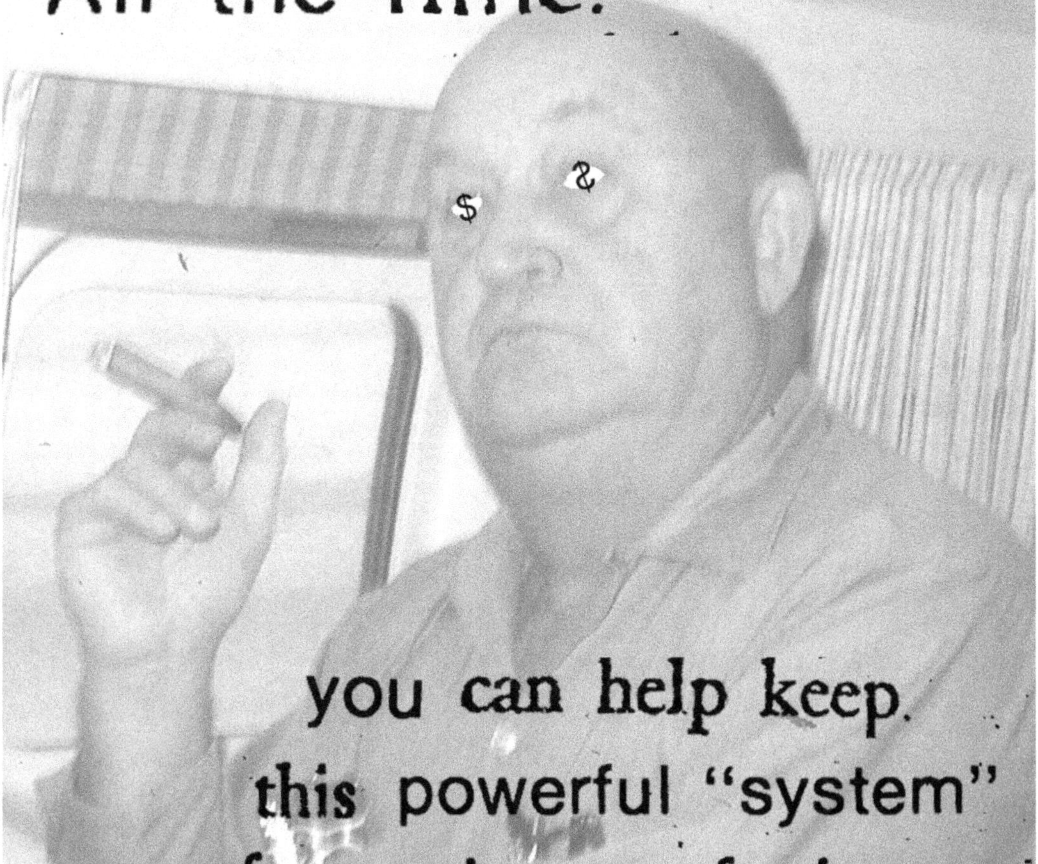

you can help keep
this powerful "system"
from going out of existence.

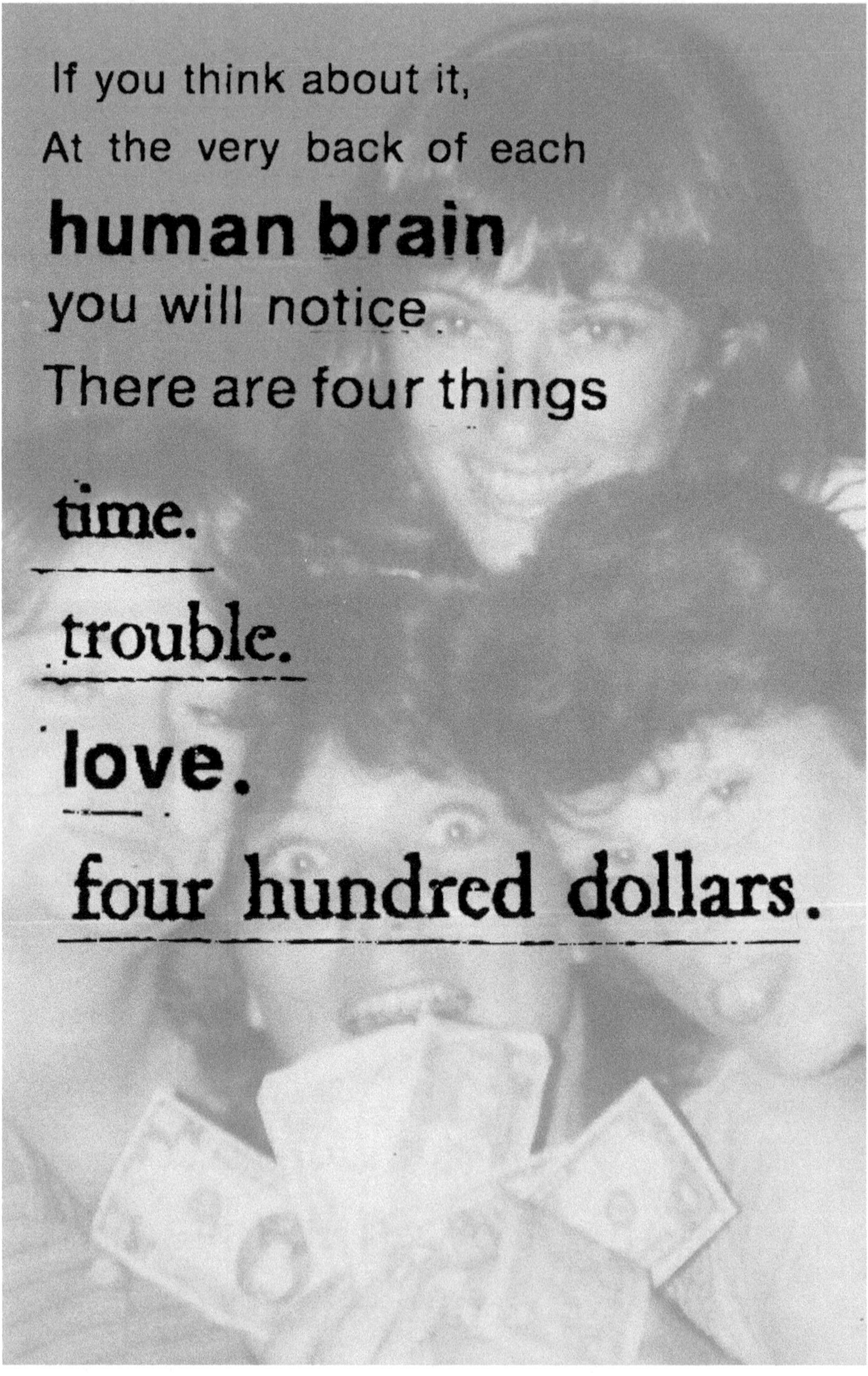

If you think about it,
At the very back of each
human brain
you will notice
There are four things

time.

trouble.

love.

four hundred dollars.

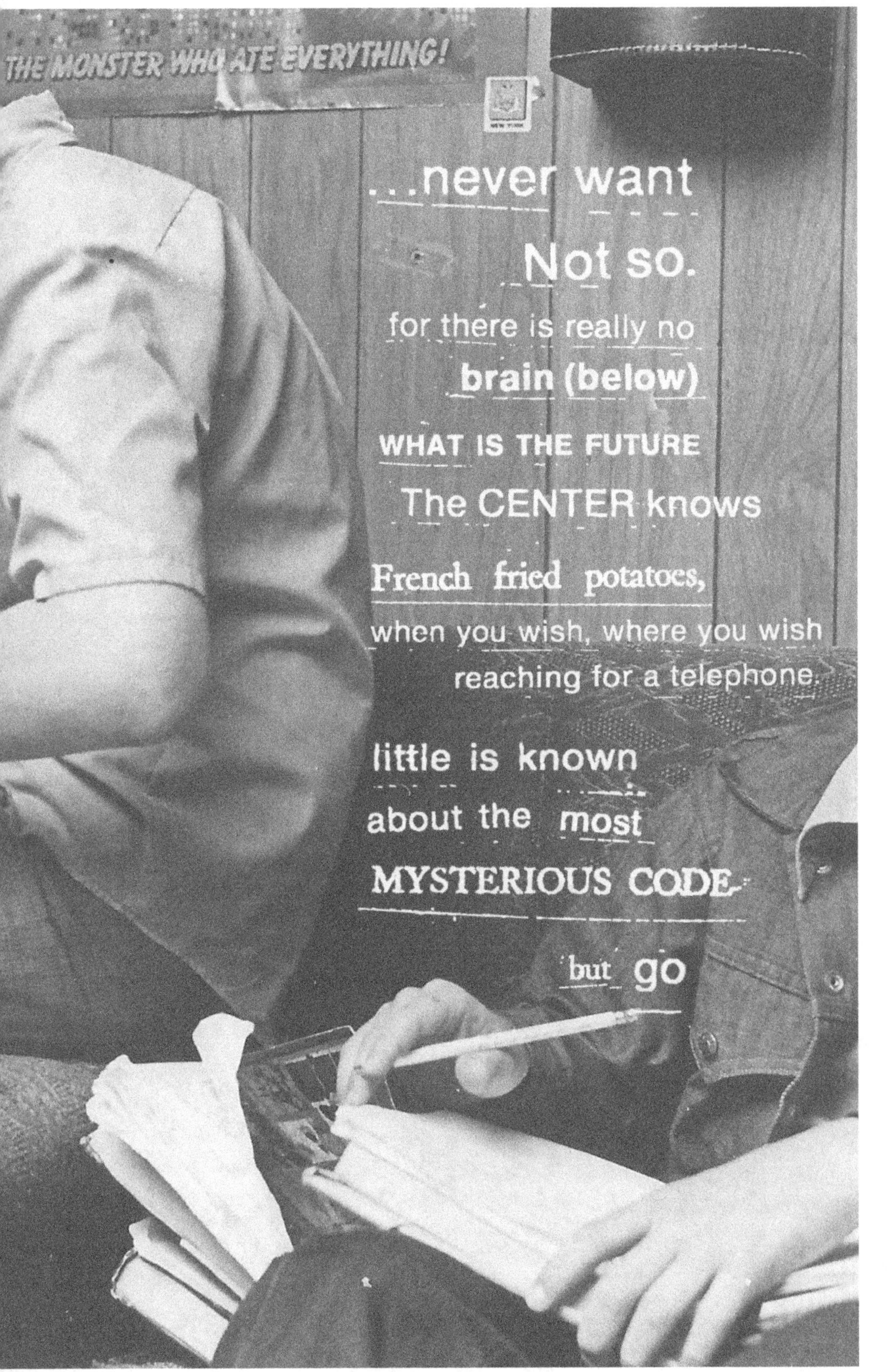
THE MONSTER WHO ATE EVERYTHING!
...never want
Not so.
for there is really no
brain (below)
WHAT IS THE FUTURE
The CENTER knows
French fried potatoes,
when you wish, where you wish
reaching for a telephone.
little is known
about the most
MYSTERIOUS CODE
but go

"Please come with me.

"Have a look at this,

Hordes of Demons

blood broken ships

frightened apart, bit by bit.

"We got into it.

Then we both said it

fully aware of it

get the power back."

Flowers are always in season

look after them.

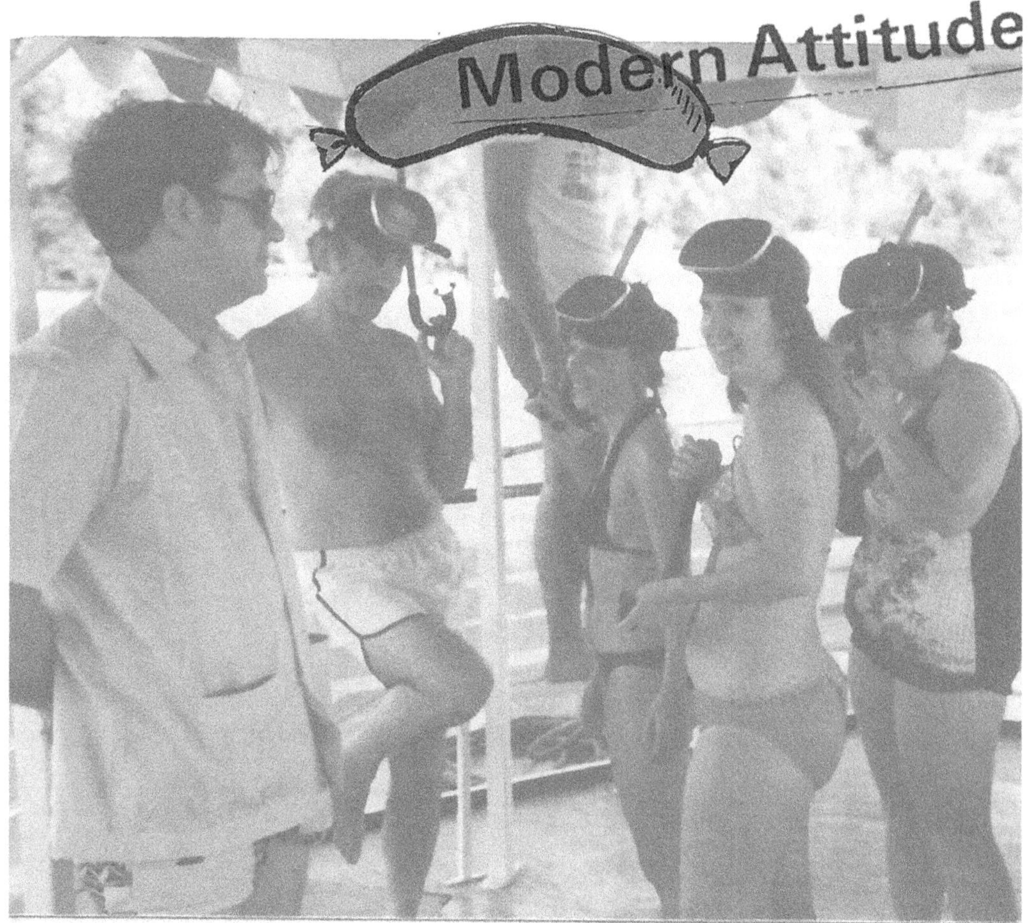

take first pill

life is not easy
We all know it
no matter how ill
you are
or
are not
or
were
or
will be ,

all will go well;

keep a watchful eye on
the clocks working inside
those frightened Shadows in the Mind
who are still looking for a solution.

They wonder if they are missing out on
something important

and they are.

Most people die in the early morning.

he wonders if he will.

put the light out and go to sleep.

take last pill

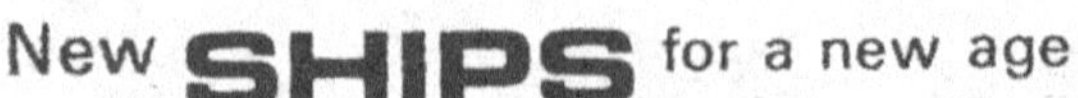

READY FOR ANYTHING ships

Finding the Way

MOVING A MOUNTAIN THE SIZE OF THE EARTH

**Keeping Up
with the World
by Remote Control**

new **Ships on the
Assembly Line**

INSTRUMENTS OF unseen terror and freedom,

SHOOTING THE SUN WITH **Longer Guns**

TURNING THE SCREWS

DOWN THE CHUTE

CLEARING THE WAY FOR FOOD

ILL-FATED **SHIPS**

MAN-MADE killers FIGHTING
man-made storms TO THE FINISH

the next ship is just beginning to take shape.

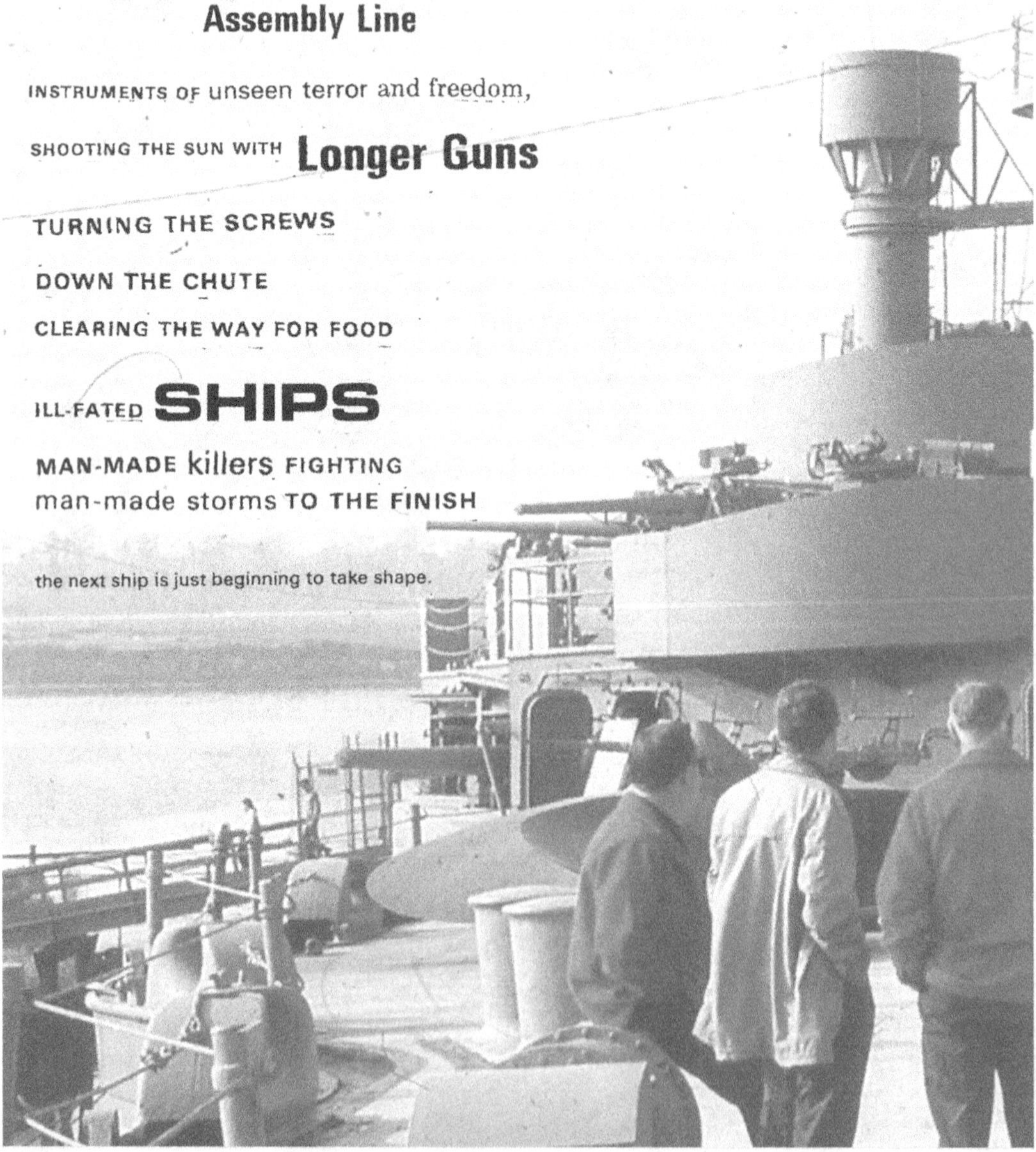

Imagine time turned back

and predict some things about the future.

Look at that.

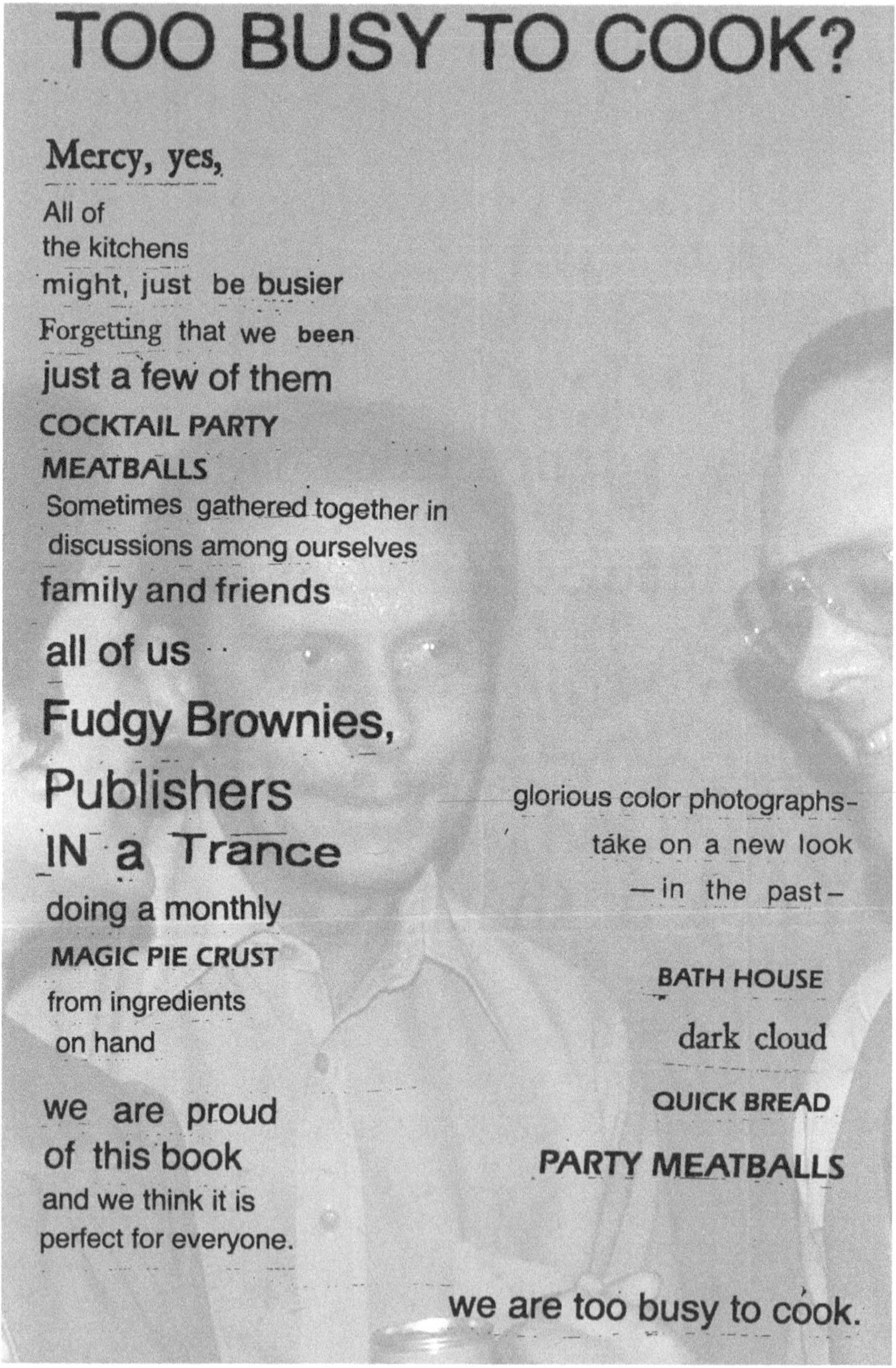

TOO BUSY TO COOK?

Mercy, yes,

All of
the kitchens
might, just be busier
Forgetting that we been
just a few of them
COCKTAIL PARTY
MEATBALLS
Sometimes gathered together in
discussions among ourselves
family and friends

all of us

Fudgy Brownies,

Publishers
IN a Trance
doing a monthly
MAGIC PIE CRUST
from ingredients
on hand

we are proud
of this book
and we think it is
perfect for everyone.

glorious color photographs-
take on a new look
— in the past —

BATH HOUSE
dark cloud
QUICK BREAD
PARTY MEATBALLS

we are too busy to cook.

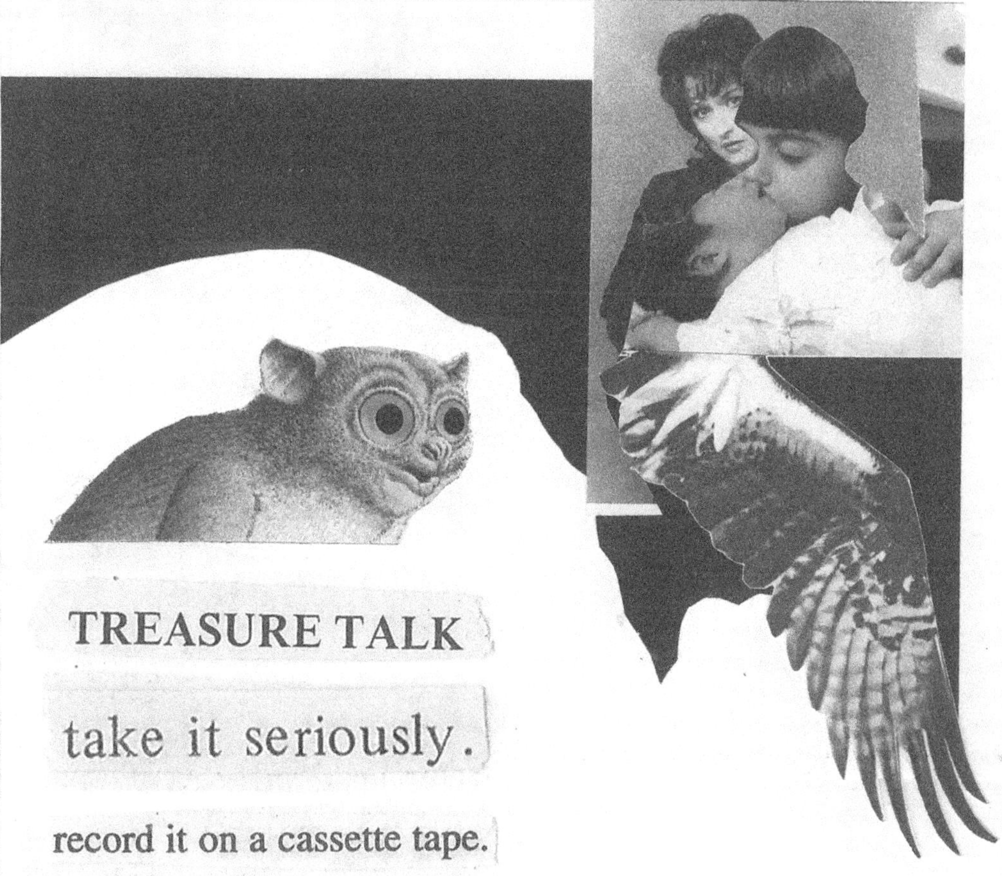

TREASURE TALK

take it seriously.

record it on a cassette tape.

every dialogue
wastes memories.

Air is dirty and often cold.

Communicating
becomes very stupid

to the point where we
pass it off as nonsense.

9 You have
made an eyeball,
filled with wonder and meaning
, but among the commonest
body parts in any magazine.

just outside A speck of dust grew larger
for the people who brought us
from the sun to The small Man

and every thing that would destroy him.

3 Think about this.

8 Yes, good people
do bad things;
like vicious animals,
over and over again

This is shown clear
on television programs

13 Today people talk a lot
say the same things
For example,
the governments
the place where they live
future life
the good things they do.
sufferings might end,
looks like.

stop for a moment and think.

If you really want to,

you will find

hearts of people

need to fear

something.

How good it is

to know the truth.

12 Think of it.

After Armageddon,

THE DEAD ARE BROUGHT BACK TO LIFE

and then visit racetracks
they watch movies
in a very deep sleep,
Like obedient sheep,
They will buy anything
this old system can bring!

But the people who live
will cease to exist.
NO MORE SICKNESS,
Everyone *is* doing it.

even if God will not listen to us,
we will be remembered
by this wicked system

What a thrill it will be

THE UNDERGROUND RESERVOIR

myths and legends
make it easy to deal with
the riches of
Man-made Arteries
balanced against
A Ponderous
Underground Flow
with nowhere else to Go

you burn it or stick pins through it
at many different places
Taming THE mysterious

a number of years fall,
to mark the hours
– that do not exist.
human being is not what life is

Is there **a magic wand**
to take us to the stars.
and out-of-doors,
to be far more ?

What Do You Think?

Every soul returns to that reservoir

Making the Water
Fit to Drink

Now think:

"All that your hand finds to do,
at any time and at any place
will get sick, grow old and die.

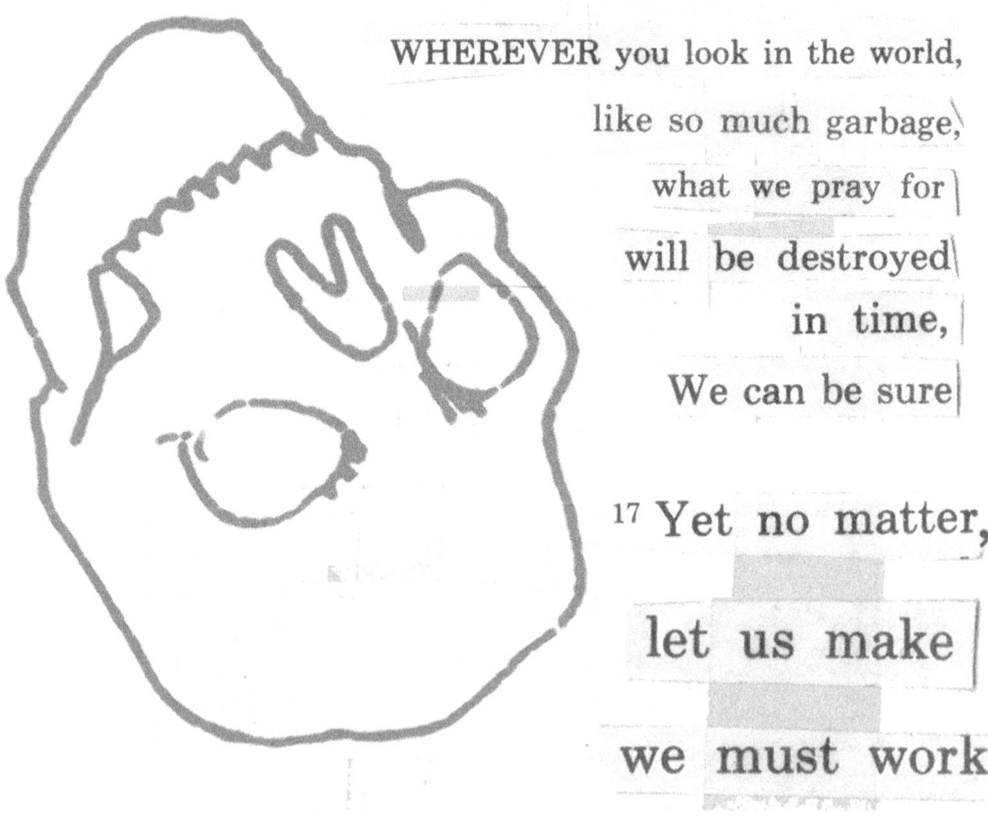

WHEREVER you look in the world,
like so much garbage,
what we pray for
will be destroyed
in time,
We can be sure

17 Yet no matter,
let us make
we must work

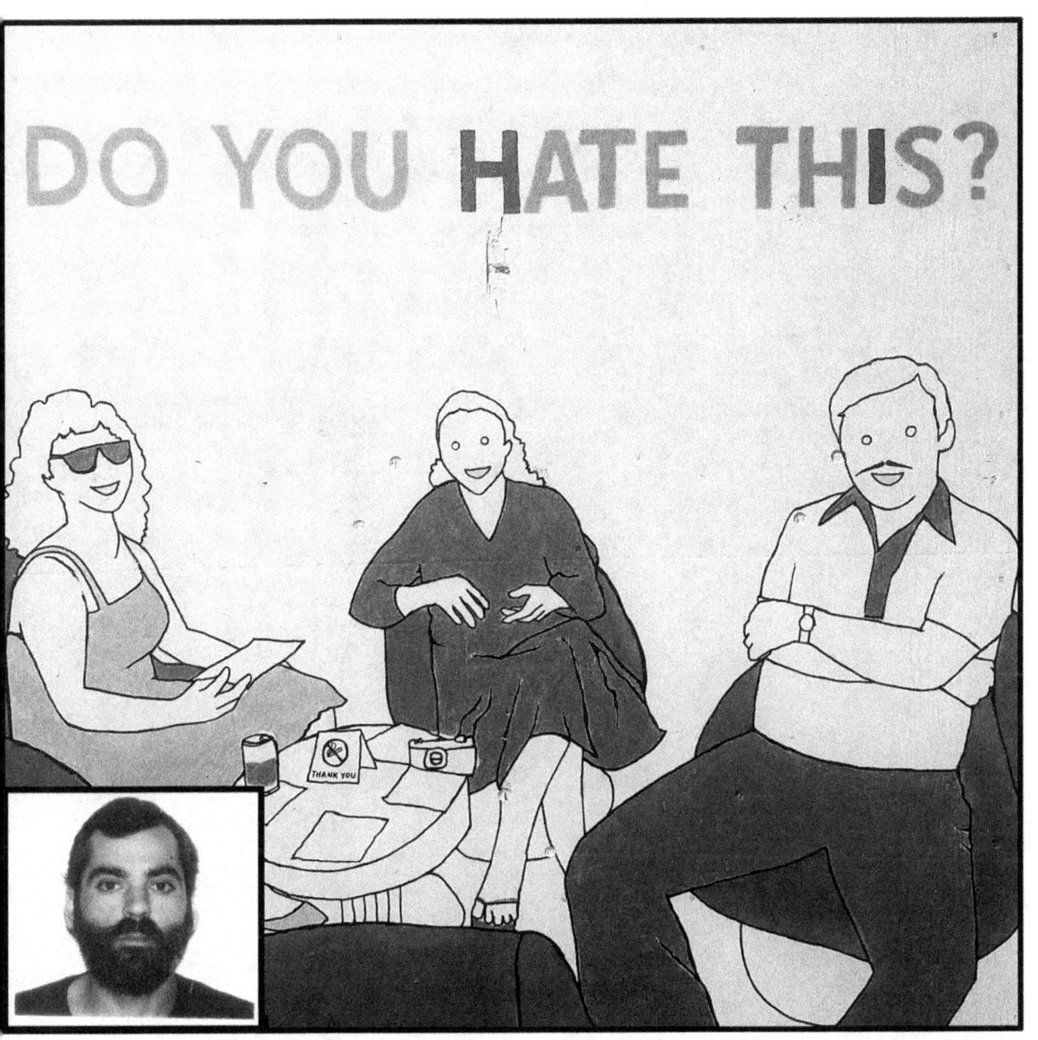

YOU CAN SUBSCRIBE TO
OFF WHITE BY AHK
AT
PATREON.COM/OFFWHITEBYAHK

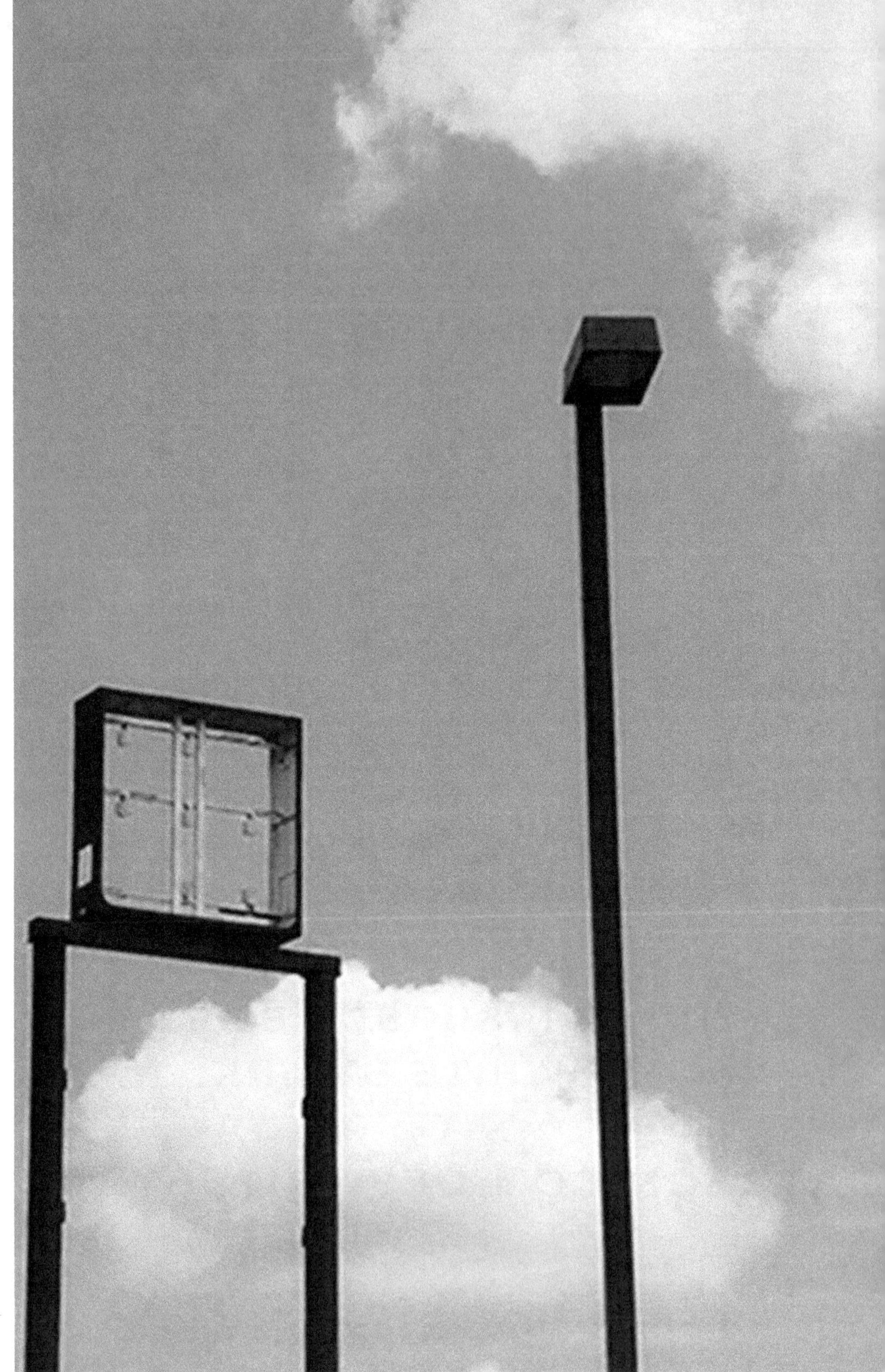

www.ingramcontent.com/pod-product-compliance
Lightning Source LLC
LaVergne TN
LVHW050611100826
845148LV00015B/3217

* 9 7 8 1 7 3 7 4 7 5 5 0 7 *